Postwar Rolls-Royce and Bentley

·A Concise Buying Guide·

Barry D. Cooney

Cooney-Taylor Publishing Inc.
Portland, Oregon, U.S.A.

First Published 1984
Cooney-Taylor Publishing Inc.
Portland, Oregon, U.S.A.

Printed in the United States of America
Library of Congress Catalogue Card Number 84-70081
ISBN 0-916117-00-6

Production/Rob Taylor
Typesetting/Harrison Typesetting, Inc.
Graphic Design/Paul C. Clark

ACKNOWLEDGEMENTS

The author would like to record his sincere appreciation to the following persons and organizations for their support and worthy contributions to the production of this book: Hermann Albers, Paul Clark, Kathleen Cooney, Doris Dorsey, Mark Heininge, Donna Oberg, Ted Reich and of course Rolls-Royce Motors, Limited.

Photo sources are gratefully acknowledged as listed below: Clyde Cassady, page 132; John deCampi, pages 84, 113 bottom right, 133 bottom right and left, 134, 135 bottom left, 136 bottom, 137 top and bottom right; Ken Karger, page 113 top; Rolls-Royce Motors, Limited, pages 81, 85, 127; Tom Solley, page 69; cover shot by Tom Stewart. All other photos are from the Theodore E. Reich photo archive.

The works of many of these photographers have appeared in various publications over the years. Accordingly, we apologize in advance if we have infringed upon anyone's copyright.

PREFACE

This book is intended to provide a basic understanding of the Rolls-Royce and Bentley motor cars produced since World War II. We will give a brief and concise description of each model in the three chassis groupings. A specification chart will be provided for each model which will include production figures where available. An investment potential rating will be assigned to each car, taking into consideration rarity, desirability, and past appreciation performance. We shall avoid delving into the history and mystique of this most interesting company, as that material has been well covered in many books previously published. Experienced owners of Rolls-Royce and Bentleys have found their enjoyment of ownership enhanced by reading and owning books about the marque. A bibliography appears at the end of this volume naming some of the titles currently available.

Rolls-Royce and Bentley clubs, of which a listing is provided, offer the camaraderie of association with fellow enthusiasts, a source of technical information, assistance in maintenance and restoration, and a market place for cars, spare parts and literature. I heartily recommend membership in one or more of them.

Generally speaking, body parts and virtually all mechanical components for post-war cars with factory coachwork are available through Rolls-Royce franchised dealers and many of the reputable after-market suppliers and service shops. Some of these are listed in chapter 25 for your reference, with the caveat that such a list is subject to constant change for a variety of reasons.

The company's policy since World War II has been to produce basically two Rolls-Royce chassis types. The large chassis (Silver Wraith, Phantom IV, Phantom V, and Phantom VI) were offered only with custom built coachwork from various manufacturers, and tended to carry larger and more formal, limousine-type bodies. You will discover however, that there are exceptions to virtually every rule in this book, as Rolls-Royce has traditionally been one of the few companies from which one could order nearly anything he wanted in the way of a custom-built motor car. The smaller chassis were offered with Rolls-Royce factory-built coachwork, usually of the more compact owner-driver variety, although there were a number of these chassis sent to custom coach-builders to be fitted with special bodies.

Since the war Bentleys have been, with little exception, the same motor car as their corresponding model Rolls-Royce. Both the Bentley Mark VI and R-type are sister cars to the Rolls-Royce Silver Dawn, and the S1, S2 and S3 Bentleys find their exact counterparts in the Rolls-Royce Silver Clouds I, II and III. In precisely the same manner, Bentley T-type and T-2 correspond to the Silver Shadow and Silver Shadow II, as does today's Bentley Mulsanne to the Rolls-Royce Silver Spirit. The Corniche has always been available as either a Rolls-

Royce or Bentley. The one major exception to this policy was the Bentley Continental, which differed somewhat in chassis specifications and was fitted with bodies built by outside firms. This model was offered to the customer desiring a more sporting automobile suitable for higher speed "continental touring" and followed in the tradition of the fine Bentley "Silent Sportscars" offered by Rolls-Royce between 1933 and 1940, and the exciting vintage sportscars produced by the original Bentley Motors (1919-1931) prior to its acquisition by Rolls-Royce in 1931.

We shall now discuss the differences between a coachbuilt car, to which is fitted a body made by an outside firm, and a car carrying a Rolls-Royce factory built body, hereafter referred to as a Standard Steel Saloon (read: "sedan"). The Standard Steel cars are far more readily available as they were the company's most widely produced product. These cars carried very handsome coachwork in standard or long wheelbase versions, and were made of a steel body shell fitted with aluminum alloy bonnet (hood), doors, and boot lid (trunk). The main difficulty with these steel-bodied cars is their serious tendency to rust. This is especially evident in cars from the eastern United States and those brought in from Great Britain owing to the practice of salting icy roads in winter. The advantages of the Standard Steel Saloons are that they usually cost less to buy than a coachbuilt car, are less prone to small dings and dents, and that virtually all body components, trim and glass are readily available.

Coachbuilt cars are generally of all-aluminum alloy construction, and while this eliminates the problem of rust, some corrosion between contacting metal panels may take place on cars from geographic locales with weather conditions which tend to rust a steel body. Another advantage to a coachbuilt car is exclusivity. Since these cars were handmade in small numbers, you won't be seeing yourself on every street corner although that is seldom a problem in a Rolls-Royce or Bentley anyway, unless you happen to be in Beverly Hills or Palm Springs. These cars often feature body styling, detailing, and luxury trim not found on the standard cars. A disadvantage is that should someone plow into your beautiful limited production coachbuilt body, you may have a difficult time finding the necessary pieces to repair it, as well as craftsmen capable of doing quality work on aluminum panels.

In the post-war period Rolls-Royce has used but two basic engines. The first was an F-Head, inline six cylinder which, upon introduction in 1946, displaced four and a quarter litres. This engine was enlarged to four and a half litres in 1951 and finally to four point nine litres in 1955. Compression and horsepower were raised accordingly over the years. Late 1959 saw the introduction of the 6¼ litre aluminum V-8 engines, Rolls-Royce's first V-8 since 1905. This replaced the highly successful sixes after their production run of nearly thirty-eight years, during which time basically the same design was used. The V-8's displacement was enlarged to six and three quarter litres in 1970 and this is the engine which is in use today, although detail refinement continues to take place.

The transition from the six cylinder to the V-8 engine took place with introduction in 1959 of the SII series of Silver Clouds and Bentleys, identical in virtually all other respects to the SIs which they replaced. In attempting to decide which engine series to own one must balance the economy of running and repair costs of the six cylinder against the power and performance of the V-8. Fuel consumption for the six generally runs in the mid to higher teens—with the lightweight R-type Continentals occasionally achieving numbers in the twenties—while the V-8 cars are usually in the 11 to 13 MPG bracket. This writer feels that both engines are comparably smooth running when properly tuned. Rolls-Royce products are extremely robust and long-lived; seldom will you hear of a mechanical failure other than those caused by neglect or poor maintenance procedures.

Your investment will be substantial whatever model you decide upon, and the best way to avoid a bad purchase is to do some planning and research before taking the plunge. Do not be in a hurry; remember the old adage "buy in haste, regret at leisure" applies well to the exotic car market. Over the years I have become firmly convinced that "bargain fixer-uppers" are seldom that. In most cases the buyer invests twice the money and work that he had anticipated, and ends up with as much money in a questionably refurbished car as it would have taken to have bought a good one initially. A bad investment of that type can seldom be recouped. Make it your objective to find the finest car that your knowledge and ability—as well as your pocket book—will allow; pay the premium price if you must, and usually in a year or two you will look back upon the purchase as a bargain. Remember that premium cars become more scarce with every year that passes.

Aside from the obvious things to avoid, such as abused, rusty or mechanically poor cars, I advise buyers to stay away from a car which has been altered or modified, other than in a minor way. For example, a neatly installed modern radio might be acceptable. But engine swaps and suspension changes are not only unnecessary, but dramatically reduce value. Such modifications completely destroy the integrity and character of the automobile. Avoid gaudy paint and unlikely color combinations or paint schemes. You may be assured that pearlescent and metalflake paints were never used by the factory; the same goes for Naugahyde upholstery and loop carpeting. These cars were all fitted with fine grade leather or wool broadcloth upholstery and Wilton cut-pile wool carpets.

All post-war cars were offered in both left- and right-hand drive, and on this continent left-hand drive is generally considered to be the more desirable, particularly in the later models. You will therefore find that in various models

LHD will increase the value as much as five to ten thousand dollars.

Something else to be aware of is the possibility of either deliberate or accidental misrepresentation. It is unfortunate that over the past few years it has become a fairly common practice to advertise a Bentley with a "full Rolls-Royce" conversion. Though genuine Rolls-Royce parts occasionally are used, what this usually amounts to is the fitting of a cheaply made imitation of a Rolls-Royce radiator shell and a few trim badges on a perfectly respectable Bentley. This may be done for the purpose of dazzling one's neighbors—whom one might feel would not be suitably impressed by ownership of a Bentley—or in some cases to outright misrepresent a car offered for sale, since Rolls-Royce tend to bring a higher price in some models than their Bentley counterparts. There is no reason for this sort of behavior, as Bentley is a great marque with a unique tradition and enjoys worldwide prestige and pride of ownership as fine as that of Rolls-Royce. The Bentley heritage dates from their glory days of dominating long distance sports car racing in the twenties (which included five victories at LeMans) to the elegant Bentley "Silent Sportscars" which were mentioned earlier.

Now we must touch on something which is far more devious, the so-called "Rolls-Royce Vanden Plas Princess Conversion". The Princess was a relatively low priced Austin based limousine which had no connection with Rolls-Royce, other than the fact that the engines, which were of smaller displacement and to less exacting specifications than those used in Rolls-Royce motorcars, were purchased from the Company. These B-range military engines were produced by a division of Rolls-Royce under contract with BMC for the Princess limousines. From time to time these cars are fitted with real or fake Rolls-Royce radiator shells and advertised as a "Rolls-Royce Princess Limousine." This is absolutely fraudulent and should be avoided at any price, if what you desire to own is a Rolls-Royce.

Armed with these caveats and having perused this book, and as many others on the subject as you can lay your hands on, as well as talking to Rolls-Royce and Bentley owners and club members, you will now hopefully, be prepared to make a wise purchase.

There are basically three groups of cars in the post war period, each offering its own individual attributes. First the large chassis Rolls-Royce offered strictly with custombuilt coachwork; second is the smaller chassis production cars which were available as either a Rolls-Royce or Bentley and generally with factory-built standard steel coachwork; finally the sleek Continental series Bentleys. It is my sincere wish that this book will help you acquire a fine example of one of these cars. Once you have made your purchase you will enjoy a pride of ownership and a joy of motoring the like of which few automobiles can provide.

TABLE OF CONTENTS

GLOSSARY OF TERMS

ALLWEATHER OR CONVERTIBLE SEDAN—A four door convertible.

BADGE ENGINEERING—A term which refers to marketing the same automobile under two, or more names by simply changing the name on the label or badge.

BONNET—The hood or metal panel over the engine.

BOOT—The trunk.

COACHBUILT—A body which was built by an outside firm, other than the company which built the chassis. Usually handcrafted in small lots.

DAMPERS—Shock absorbers.

DROPHEAD COUPE OR DHC—A convertible with roll-up windows.

FACIA—The dashboard or instrument panel.

FIXEDHEAD COUPE OR FHC—A hardtop coupe, non-opening.

HEAD—British for automobile roof.

HOOD—Convertible top.

LANDAULETTE—A limousine in which the portion of the roof behind the rear doors folds down.

LIGHT—Refers to a side window other than a front vent.

LIMOUSINE—A very large enclosed four door body with a glass division; usually with occasional seats in the rear.

MASCOT—The ornament mounted on the radiator cap.

MONOCOQUE—A form of chassis construction in which the body sheet metal makes up the center section of the frame.

OVERRIDERS—Bumper guards.

SALOON—British term for a sedan.

SEDANCA COUPE—A four seat coupe in which the roof above the drivers compartment can be removed or folded back into the coachwork.

SEDANCA DE VILLE—A limousine or saloon in which the roof can be opened as in the Sedanca Coupe.

SEMI-COACHBUILT—For our purpose refers to cars, particularly the Silver Cloud series, which prior to delivery were sent to Park Ward or H.J. Mulliner to have the original body shell modified to the long wheelbase version or the two door convertible.

SHOOTING BRAKE OR ESTATE—Station wagon.

SPATS—Fender skirts.

THREE POSITION TOP—A convertible top which can be used either closed, opened just above the drivers compartment, or fully opened.

TOURING LIMOUSINE—A compact limousine, usually with division but without occasional seats.

TRAFFICATORS—Flip-out turn signal arms, usually illuminated.

WINGS—Fenders.

INVESTMENT RATING

The rating system is based on a scale of one to ten points with ten being the most desirable. A scale of this breadth is necessary due to the diverse nature of these cars. It also allows for a point range on the Silver Wraith, Phantom V and Phantom VI which can vary in value depending upon the different bodies with which they may be fitted. The Phantom IV is excluded, because it is so rare and valuable that coachwork differences do not affect its desirability.

Of the remaining cars, the ratings will reflect values when fitted with the standard factory coachwork. The Bentley Continentals are rated with the most often-fitted saloon bodies. Rare or exceptional coachwork can obviously alter value in any chassis type.

For the sake of comparison we assume all vehicles to be in equal and average condition, requiring perhaps some detailing or minor repairs, but with no major defects. Past appreciation performance as well as present desirability and scarcity are among the many factors that have been considered in assessing the values. But when all is said and done, the things that you must consider are your own preferences and the actual condition of the automobile in question.

SILVER WRAITH: 4-8

PHANTOM IV: 10

PHANTOM V: 6-9

PHANTOM VI: 7-9

SILVER DAWN: 7

SILVER CLOUD I—S1: R 6, B 5

SILVER CLOUD II—S2: R 5, B 4

SILVER CLOUD III—S3: R 7, B 6

SILVER SHADOW—T-TYPE: 6

CORNICHE: 8

CAMARGUE: 8

SILVER SHADOW II—T2: 7

SILVER SPIRIT—MULSANNE: 7

MARK VI: 4-6

R-TYPE: 4-6

R-TYPE CONTINENTAL: 9

S1 CONTINENTAL: 8

S2 CONTINENTAL: 7-8

S3 CONTINENTAL: 7-8

TURBO MULSANNE: 8-9

Introduction to Coachbuilders

World War II signaled the end of many handcrafts; among these was the art of coachbuilding automobile bodies. Nearly two-thirds of the firms producing specialty bodies in England before the war did not go back into production after hostilities had ceased in 1945. So we find that while there were a number of small firms making the occasional special body for a Rolls-Royce or Bentley, there remained only five firms building bodies in any numbers on these chassis. Of these five, Freestone and Webb, which was formed in 1923, was to last only until 1958. The next to discontinue production was the old and well-established firm of Hooper and Company (Coachbuilders) Ltd., formed in 1805. They last exhibited at the 1959 motor show in London and produced no other examples after that.

Park Ward, which was initially founded in 1919, formed a close liaison with Rolls-Royce and by the thirties, ninety percent of their production was on that chassis. In 1939 the firm was purchased by Rolls-Royce Ltd. After the war they continued producing bodies for what was now their parent company although they did produce some bodies for the Alvis concern.

The firm of H.J. Mulliner and Company began life in Brook Street, Mayfair, London in the year 1900. They built many interesting and high quality bodies, including the innovative High Vision Saloon before the war and their very successful lightweight bodies on the standard and Continental chassis after the war. As coachbuilding diminished later in the fifties an approach was made which resulted in the company being acquired by Rolls-Royce in 1959. In 1961 Rolls-Royce Ltd. merged their two coachbuilding firms into one, bearing the name H.J. Mulliner-Park Ward Ltd., which still carries on the tradition by building the bodies for the Corniche series as well as the Phantom VI and Camargue.

One of the outstanding coachbuilders of both the pre- and post-war periods was the firm of James Young Ltd. They designed many new ideas into their work, including their patented parallel-opening doors of the late thirties. The bodies which they built on the Rolls-Royce Phantom V are surely to be found on anyone's list of most beautiful cars produced during that era. Despite all this the handwriting was on the wall, and in 1967, as Rolls-Royce was fully in production with the chassisless, monocoque-construction Silver Shadow and T-Type Bentley, James Young ceased coachbuilding activities, which had been their mainstay for over one hundred years.

The following is a listing of some of the other firms which produced specialty bodies on the Rolls-Royce and Bentley chassis during the post-war years:

Abbott	Henri Chapron
Beutler	Inskip
Duncan	Pininfarina
Facel-Metallon	Ramseier
Figoni-Falaschi	Rippon
Franay	Saoutchik
Ghia	Vanden Plas
Graber	Vignale
Gurney Nutting	Vincents of Reading
Harold Radford	Windovers
Harwood	Worblaufen.

SILVER WRAITH

1946-1959

I

The Silver Wraith was first introduced in late 1946. It is unique in that it has that elegant prewar look and yet possesses the driving characteristics of today's modern cars. This is a very large car by present standards but can be comfortably driven by almost anyone due to the ease of steering and controls as well as the silky-smooth gear change.

While considered old-fashioned in some ways at introduction there is nothing that could match its detail refinement when compared to its contemporaries.

The earliest cars can be identified visually by the divided bonnet sides, which in 1947 became one-piece. What lay under that bonnet was a redesigned version of the pre-war inline six cylinder which had been used in the Bentleys and small-chassis Rolls-Royce. The cylinder head design was changed to an F configuration, consisting of an overhead inlet and side exhaust-valves. This was done in the interest of enlarging valve size as well as displacement. Initially the upper portion of the cylinder bores were chromium plated, but by 1950, as some cars began to accumulate high mileage, it became apparent that this was not the most satisfactory arrangement. (The cylinder wear became very rapid as the .0015″ thick chromium plating wore through). This method was then abandoned, and subsequent engines were fitted with a short, pressed-in

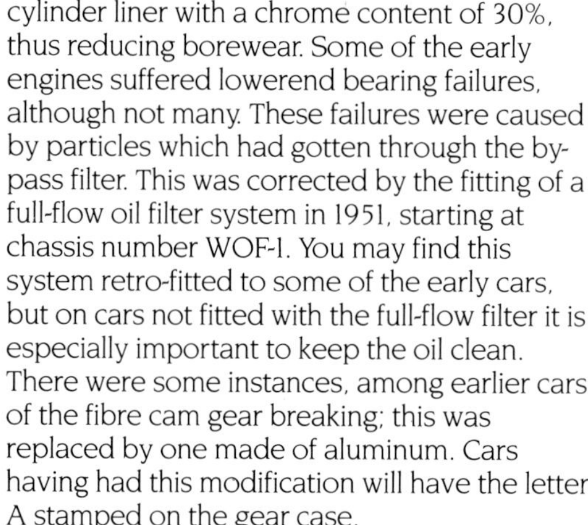

cylinder liner with a chrome content of 30%, thus reducing borewear. Some of the early engines suffered lowerend bearing failures, although not many. These failures were caused by particles which had gotten through the by-pass filter. This was corrected by the fitting of a full-flow oil filter system in 1951, starting at chassis number WOF-1. You may find this system retro-fitted to some of the early cars, but on cars not fitted with the full-flow filter it is especially important to keep the oil clean. There were some instances, among earlier cars of the fibre cam gear breaking; this was replaced by one made of aluminum. Cars having had this modification will have the letter A stamped on the gear case.

The cooling system, at four gallons, is more than adequate but it must be remembered that the Silver Wraiths, along with the Phantom IV's, are the only post-war Rolls-Royces to use the thermostatically controlled radiator shutters carried over from the pre-war period. It is essential that the shutters function properly. Later models were fitted with fixed shutters and modern-type thermostat.

In 1951, as the engine was enlarged to 4½ litres, the wheelbase was stretched six inches in order to accommodate larger coachwork. In 1952 an automatic transmission was offered as an option. This gearbox was manufactured in

Investment Rating: 4-8

its entirety by Rolls-Royce under license from General Motors on the GM Hydramatic design patent. The four-speed automatic, while not the smoothest shifting gearbox ever devised, has served well thru the years and was used until 1968 when it was replaced by a three-speed automatic with torque converter. You may note that while the four-speed automatic did not have a "park" position, one may be effected by selecting reverse and shutting off the engine. This engages two gears simultaneously and will hold the car in position.

In 1955 the engine was enlarged again. This time to 4.9 litres and the automatic transmission became standard equipment. The single carburator system which had been used from the beginning was changed to twin 1¾" S.U.s in 1956, but 1957 saw a sizeable jump in power with the fitting of 2" S.U.s and an increase in compression to 8.0:1.

During its thirteen year production run the Silver Wraith was fitted with widely differing styles of coachwork. These varied from relatively compact (considering their chassis size) coupes and convertibles, to huge 7/8 passenger limousines and stately landaulettes. Coachwork is something which one should examine very carefully. The standard practice was to build a wooden framework for the body; the aluminum paneling was then formed over this. Coachwork of this type can be vulnerable to penetration of moisture and cars with extensive wood rot should be avoided. This is a major repair project and can be very costly. A good way to check for wood rot is to examine the way the doors hang and how the boot lid fits. If, upon opening, a door drops measurably as it leaves its sill, one should examine the car further. Other areas to watch are the running boards, if the car is so equipped, and around the back window.

Regardless of whether it be an early or a late chassis, no matter what body style might happen to be fitted, the Silver Wraith, perhaps more than any other model produced since the war, represents the smooth, silent grace that is Rolls-Royce. During the production run of this car we sadly witnessed the ending of an era of craftsmanship and individuality. These cars eventually became elegant dinosaurs, no longer fitting into an era of look-alike transportation and mass production.

Silver Wraith: *Hooper saloon.*

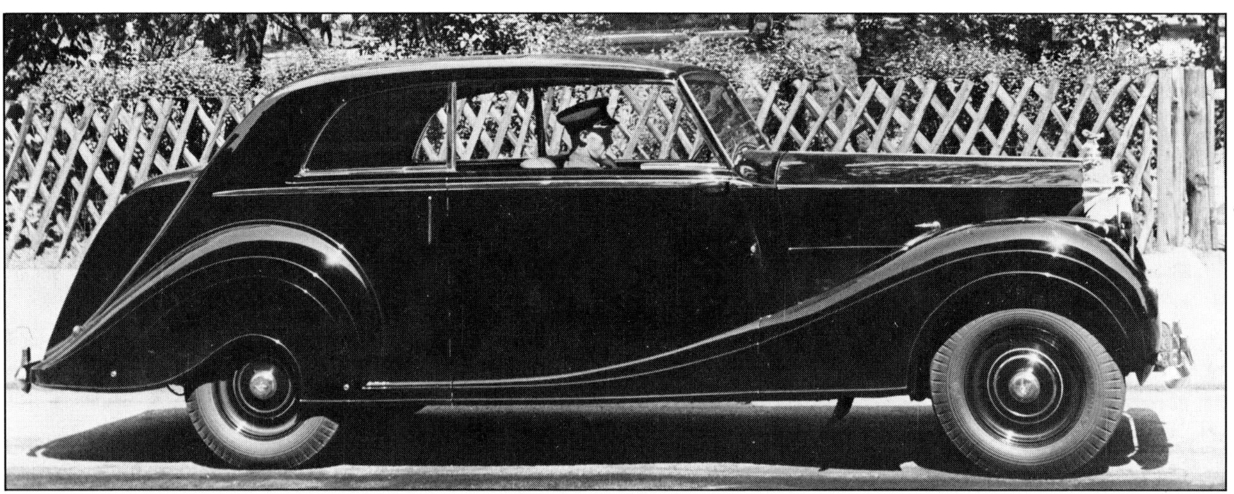

Silver Wraith: *James Young's handsome design called the saloon Coupe was a carryover from pre-war days. This example is on a very early chassis identified by split bonnet sides and plain wheelcovers.*

Silver Wraith: *Freestone and Webb saloon with division. 1948 Model.*

Silver Wraith: *James Young fixedhead coupe on an early chassis.*

ENGINE

Type: F-head inline six cylinder

Bore & stroke, displacement: 1946, 3½″×4½″, 4257 cc; 1951, 3⅝″×4½″, 4566 cc; 1955, 3¾″×4½″, 4887 cc

Compression ratio: 1946, 6.4:1; 1952, 6.4:1 or 6.75:1; 1953, 6.75:1; 1957, 8.0:1

Carburetion: SWB models, dualthroat downdraft Stromberg; 1952 sidedraft Zenith LWB models downdraft zenith; 1956 twin 1¾″ S.U.s; 1957 Twin 2″ S.U.s

CHASSIS AND DRIVETRAIN

Transmission: 4-speed manual, synchro on 2nd, 3rd & 4th, ratios 2.98:1, 2.02:1, 1.34:1, 1:1; 1952 4-speed automatic optional, ratios 3.82:1, 2.63:1, 1.45:1, 1:1

Clutch: Single 10″ dry-plate: 1947 11″ heavy type.

Final drive: SWB 3.73:1; 1951 3.42:1 optional; LWB 3.73:1 or 3.42:1; 1955 with automatic transmission 4.25:1; 1956 3.89:1

Suspension: Front, independent coil springs, hydraulic dampers; Rear, half-elliptic springs with controllable hydraulic dampers

Steering: Cam and roller, 1950 modified geometry; 1956 power assisted

Brakes: Front, hydraulic; Rear, mechanical. Mechanical servo assist

GENERAL

Wheelbase: .... SWB 127″; LWB 133″

Track: Front: .... SWB 58″; LWB 58″

Rear: .... SWB 60″; LWB 64″

Tires: .... SWB 6.50×17″; LWB 7.50×16″

Weight: .... Approx. 3200 lbs. for SWB, chassis only

Number produced: .... SWB 1144; LWB 639

Silver Wraith: *James Young touring limousine. Note similarity to H.J. Mulliner's design.*

Silver Wraith: *H.J. Mulliner touring limousine. This car and the above James Young version were produced in 1949.*

Silver Wraith: *H.J. Mulliner drop-head coupe. 1951 chassis WGC 48.*

Silver Wraith: *Franay drophead coupe. 1949 chassis WYA69.*

Silver Wraith: *H.J. Mulliner sedanca de ville.*

Silver Wraith: *Park Ward saloon. 6-light version.*

Silver Wraith: *James Young saloon.*

Silver Wraith: *James Young sedanca de ville. Chassis LWVH41.*

Silver Wraith: *Hooper saloon. This handsome design was known as the Teviot III.*

Silver Wraith: *Freestone and Webb saloon.*

Silver Wraith: *H.J. Mulliner touring limousine.*

Silver Wraith: *H.J. Mulliner seven-passenger limousine.*

Silver Wraith: *Hooper touring limousine. Note radio antenna mounted horizonally under left door sill.*

Silver Wraith: *Hooper touring limousine showing the development from the above flowing lines which in later phases came to be known as "Empress" styling.*

Silver Wraith: *Park Ward touring limousine.*

Silver Wraith: *H.J. Mulliner called this design a Sports Limousine.*

Silver Wraith: *Hooper seven-passenger limousine on a late chassis.*

Silver Wraith: *interior view of the Hooper seven-passenger limousine.*

Silver Wraith: *James Young seven-passenger limousine on a late chassis.*

Silver Wraith: *saloon body by the French firm of Henri Chapron on a late chassis.*

Silver Wraith: *Park Ward seven-passenger limousine.*

Silver Wraith: *Abbott drophead coupe.*

Silver Wraith: *Park Ward seven-passenger limousine; an example of the lavish interior found in some of these cars.*

ENGINE

Type: F-head inline eight cylinder

Bore & stroke, displacement: 3½″ × 4½″, 5675cc

Compression ratio: 6.4:1

Carburetion: Stromberg dual downdraft

CHASSIS AND DRIVETRAIN

Transmission: 4-speed, synchro on 2nd, 3rd and 4th; ratios 2.98:1, 2.02:1, 1.34:1, 1:1

Clutch: Single 11″ dry-plate; heavy type

Final drive: 4.25:1

Suspension: Front, independent, coil springs, hydraulic dampers; Rear, half-elliptic with controllable hydraulic dampers

Steering: Cam and roller

Brakes: Front, hydraulic; Rear, mechanical. Mechanical servo assist

GENERAL

Wheelbase:	145″
Track: Front:	58½″
Rear:	63″
Tires:	8.00×17″
Weight:	3900 lbs. for chassis only (est.)
Number produced:	18

Phantom IV: *Franay allweather 4AF22, designed as indicated on this artists rendering for The King of Saudi Arabia.*

Phantom IV: *Hooper touring limousine 4BP3.*

Phantom IV: *Hooper sedanca de ville 4AF20. Built for The Aga Khan.*

Phantom IV: *Hooper limousine.*

Phantom **IV:** *Hooper touring limousine 4BP1.*

PHANTOM V

1959-1968

3

With the passing of the Silver Wraith the time had come for those other than Heads of State, once again to be able to purchase a Phantom. This opportunity had not been available since production of the V-12 engined Phantom III had been ended by the coming of war in 1939. The introduction in late 1959 of the Phantom V coincided with the Silver Cloud II, and they shared the same V-8 powerplant and other mechanical components. The design was to remain basically unaltered throughout its production run, the major alterations taking place in 1962 with the addition of four headlights, a lower radiator and bonnet line, and the repositioning of the parking lights. These changes, along with upgraded carburetors, were carried out in order to remain current with the Silver Cloud III which was announced at that time.

The Phantom V offered a chassis which was a full twelve inches longer than the long wheelbase Silver Wraith. This provided the coach builders an ample platform upon which to erect the most elaborate example of their craft. Unfortunately, their ranks were rather diminished by this time, but this did not prevent the creation of some of the most handsome automobiles seen during the post-war years. The James Young Phantom V Touring Limousine was perhaps the most gracefully proportioned large car of this era, and was awarded a Gold Medal in the coach-building competition of the 1965 London Motor Show at Earl's Court.

The 1966 Earl's Court Show saw H.J. Mulliner-Park Ward introduce a State Landaulette in which the entire rear compartment opened to enable its passengers to stand and be more easily viewed during processions. The rear seat of this model could be raised three inches when the top was opened, should the passengers choose to increase visibility while remaining seated. With this car we once again had a Phantom suitable for Heads of State and Royalty. Other body styles offered on the Phantom V were the Seven Passenger Limousine and Sedanca de Ville by James Young. Park Ward, too, offered a seven passenger limousine, and H.J. Mulliner created several limousines and at least one five passenger saloon before the company was combined with Park Ward. Hooper and Company, which had made the test body for the Phantom V prototype, was to make but one P-V body, a limousine, before they ceased production. The late Mr. Osmond Rivers of Hooper and Company, designed and supervised the building of one other P-V by the Paris firm of Henri Chapron. A few one-off designs were produced over the years, but by 1967, of the major firms, only H.J. Mulliner-Park Ward remained, producing a seven passenger limousine, as well as the above mentioned State Landaulette.

Investment Rating: 6-9

Phantom V: Park Ward limousine, this was the earliest version by this coachbuilder on the Phantom V chassis.

The interior of the Phantom V provided among the most sumptuous accommodations available in any automobile. The chauffeur's compartment was upholstered in the finest leather and either leather or West of England woolen cloth could be specified for the rear. Folding occasional seats were fitted to most examples, and the interior woodwork and cocktail cabinets featured gorgeous inlaid veneers of the highest quality. Elaborate ladies' vanity items and gentlemens' smoking accoutrements were to be found in many.

At nearly twenty feet in overall length, this may not be the model which you would choose for daily in-town driving, but as a collector's car or for serious formal use it cannot be faulted. As large as it is, this car is most pleasant to drive with its light steering and powerful brakes, and while the coachwork may be elaborate, the mechanics are no harder to deal with than those of a Silver Cloud II or III.

In the end it could be argued whether the two or four headlight version is the more handsome, but few could argue that the Phantom V is perhaps the most luxurious way, short of a private rail car, in which one can travel across the land.

Phantom V: *James Young touring limousine fitted with optional spats and an alternative quarter-light treatment.*

Phantom V: *James Young sedanca de ville with simulated canework on the rear doors.*

Phantom V: H.J. Mulliner-Park Ward limousine, property of HM The Queen of England. Rear portion of the roof is removable, revealing a Perspex under-roof for processional use.

ENGINE

Type: Overhead valve V8

Bore & stroke, displacement: 4.1″ × 3.6″, 6230cc

Compression ratio: 8:1 or 9:1

Carburetion: Twin HD6 S.U.s

CHASSIS AND DRIVETRAIN

Transmission: 4-speed automatic, ratios 3.82:1, 2.63:1, 1.45:1, 1:1

Final drive: 3.89:1

Suspension: Front, independent, unequal length wishbones with coil springs and hydraulic dampers; Rear, asymetric semi-elliptic springs with controllable dampers

Steering: Power assisted cam and roller

Brakes: Front, hydraulic; Rear, combined hydraulic and mechanical. Mechanical servo assist. Two separate hydraulic systems and master cylinders.

GENERAL

Wheelbase: .... 144″

Track: Front: .... 61″

Rear: .... 64″

Tires: .... 8.90 × 15″

Weight: .... Approx. 5600 lbs.

Number produced: 832

Phantom V: James Young two-door saloon. Only two examples of this rare bodystyle were produced.

Phantom V: H.J. Mulliner saloon, a particularly rare model on the PV. Note family resemblance to other H.J. Mulliner coachwork.

Phantom V: *H.J. Mulliner-Park Ward limousine.*

Phantom V: *James Young seven-passenger limousine.*

PHANTOM VI

1968-PRESENT

4

The Phantom VI is the current offering by Rolls-Royce for the large chassis, coachbuilt market. The main difference between it and the Phantom V, is its use of the Silver Shadow engine and ventilation system, and the fitting of dual air conditioning units.

This model has never been federalized and is not offered for sale in the United States, but there are a few examples in this country which have been brought in privately. The Phantom VI can be visually identified by the scuttle-mounted air vents which are situated between the windscreen and the bonnet.

This model utilized the four-speed automatic transmission with its servo assist to the drum brakes until 1979 when it was replaced by the three-speed with torque-converter which had been in use on the Silver Shadow for nearly ten years. The drum brakes have remained, but the transmission-driven servo has been replaced by a twin power-brake arrangement with a single mechanical linkage. Steering continues to be of the cam and roller variety and a live axle is employed at the rear. The dual S.U. carburetors which were initially used have been deleted in favor of a single Solex 4A1 compound four-barrel.

Selecting the body for a Phantom is not what it used to be, since the coachbuilding trade is now all but gone. Mulliner-Park Ward is virtually the only one remaining who can erect coachwork upon these cars. They offer only the Seven Passenger Limousine and their State Landaulette. Construction time for one of these cars is nearly nine months as they are still built, almost entirely by hand. A buyer can specify the individual details and fittings required to suit his needs, but now most customers are corporations or governments rather than individuals.

The era of this type of automobile as private transportation may have come and gone, but it is somehow comforting to know that there is still enough demand to keep Rolls-Royce producing a few of these magnificent cars each year.

Investment Rating: 7-9

Phantom ***VI:*** *H.J. Mulliner-Park Ward State Landaulette.*

Phantom VI: H.J. Mulliner-Park *Ward limousine.*

Phantom VI: H.J. Mulliner-Park *Ward limousine. The P VI can be identified by the air intake vents on the scuttle.*

ENGINE
Type: Overhead valve V8
Bore & stroke, displacement: 4.1″×3.6″, 6230cc; 4.1″×3.9×, 6750cc
Compression ratio: 9.0:1, 8.0:1
Carburetion: Twin HD8 S.U.s; Solex 4A1 four choke

CHASSIS AND DRIVETRAIN
Transmission: 4-speed automatic, ratios 3.82:1, 2.63:1, 1.45:1, 1:1; 1979 3-speed automatic with torque converter
Final drive: 3.89:1
Suspension: Front, independent, unequal length wishbones with coil springs and hydraulic dampers; Rear, asymetric semi-elliptic springs with controllable hydraulic dampers.
Steering: Power assisted cam and roller
Brakes: Front, hydraulic drum type; Rear, combined hydraulic and mechanical drum type. Mechanical servo assist. 1979 servo deleted, replaced by two powered hydraulic and one mechanical linkage. Four wheel drums retained.

GENERAL
Wheelbase: . . . . 144″
Track: Front: . . . . 61″
Rear: . . . . 64″
Tires: . . . . 8.90×15″
Weight: . . . . 6045 lbs.
Number produced: . . . . N/A

***Phantom VI:** front interior.*

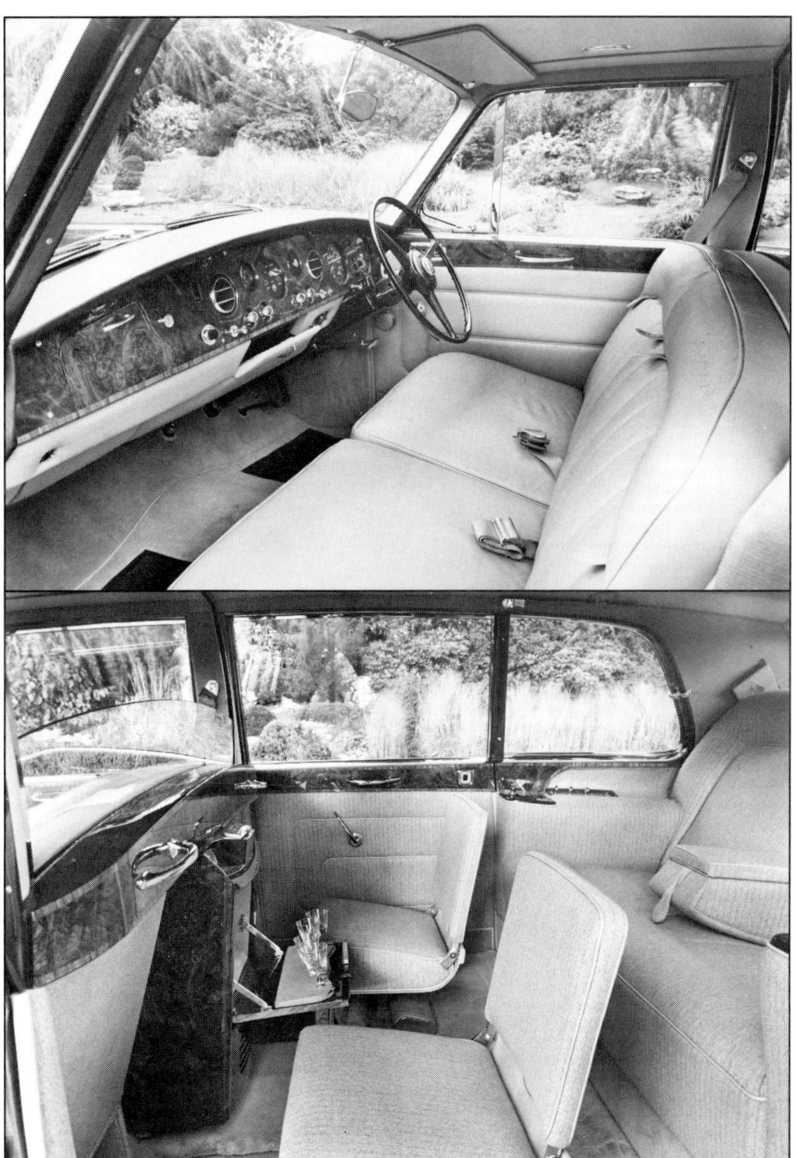

***Phantom VI:** rear interior.*

SILVER DAWN

1949-1955

5

The Silver Dawn was introduced in 1949 and aimed at the lucrative American market. The idea was to offer a smaller Rolls-Royce with factory built coachwork, less expensive than the Silver Wraith, and more appealing to the owner/driver. Thus the Mark VI Bentley, which had been in production since 1946, was fitted with a Rolls-Royce radiator shell and appropriate trim badges, then christened the Silver Dawn. Since these cars were initially created for export, nearly all early examples will be found to have left-hand drive and the accompanying column change for the four-speed gearbox. In 1952 automatic transmission became an option. The chassis was lengthened 7″ behind the rear wheels with the boot being stretched accordingly. This move coincided with the Mark VI Bentley becoming the R type, since the Silver Dawn shared a common body shell with the Bentleys.

The Silver Dawn was the first Rolls-Royce with factory built steel coachwork and is the only Standard Steel Rolls-Royce which retains the upright, dignified look of the pre-war models. Therefore, with its traditional lines and its compact (120″ wheelbase) size, it offers an attractive and usable package to the person wanting a classic looking Rolls-Royce which he can drive daily. These factors combined with the small production figures, amounting to only 760 examples total, have made this one of the faster appreciating post-war models. This popularity has led some people to succumb to the temptation of changing the appearance of their Mk.VI/R type Bentleys to that of the Silver Dawn. These fakes can be quickly detected by examining the reveal which runs from the scuttle forward along the bonnet toward the radiator shell. On the Silver Dawn the reveal reaches the radiator shell while on the Bentleys it stops about 3″ short. This rule applies to the Silver Cloud series as well.

The quality of steel available after World War II was very low and the body pressings for the cars of this era suffered accordingly. Despite the careful rustproofing measures taken by The Company, many of these cars have extensive rust. Potential trouble areas are the lower door sills, rear wheel arches, the floor of the boot, and inside the sunroof channels. Incidentally, a sunroof was fitted to all Standard Steel Silver Dawns, Mark VI Bentleys and R types, so don't allow this to be touted as something out of the ordinary when considering a car.

Investment Rating: 7

Silver Dawn: *standard steel saloon, short boot model.*

The heater, which lives under the left front seat, is minimally effective and the separate blower for defrosting the windshield is also inadequate by modern standards. One may wish to take this into consideration if he lives in a cold climate and intends to use the car for daily transportation.

The investment appreciation for the Silver Dawn, over the past ten years, has been among the very best. In 1972 prices were consistently under $10,000.00 while at the time of this writing it will likely take over $30,000.00 to own a pristine example. With that in mind, plus the fact that it is a delightful car to drive, it becomes one of the more appealing models to seek when considering the purchase of a Rolls-Royce.

Silver Dawn: standard steel saloon, side scuttle vents identify this short boot model as one of the last of that series.

ENGINE

Type: F-head inline six cylinder

Bore & stroke, displacement: 3½″×4½″, 4257cc; 1951 3⅝″×4½″, 4566cc

Compression ratio: 6.4:1; 1953 6.75:1

Carburetion: Stromberg downdraft; 1952 Zenith

CHASSIS AND DRIVETRAIN

Transmission: 4-speed manual, synchro on 2nd, 3rd and 4th, ratios 2.98:1, 2.02:1, 1.34:1, 1:1; 1952 automatic optional, ratios 3.82:1, 2.63:1, 1.45:1, 1:1

Clutch: Single 10″, dry plate; 1950 11″ light type; 1951 11″ heavy type

Final drive: 3.73:1; 1954 3.42:1

Suspension: Front, independent coil springs, hydraulic dampers; Rear, half-elliptic springs with controllable hydraulic dampers

Steering: Cam and roller, 1950 modified geometry

Brakes: Front, hydraulic; Rear, mechanical. Mechanical servo assist

GENERAL

Wheelbase: .... 120″

Track: Front: .... 56½″

Rear: .... 58⅝″

Tires: .... 6.50×16″

Weight: .... Short boot 4100 lbs.; long boot 4250 lbs.

Number produced: 760

Silver Dawn: *standard steel saloon, long boot model.*

*S**ilver Dawn:** special drophead coupe by H.J. Mulliner. Note unusual rear window treatment.*

Silver Dawn: *Park Ward drophead coupe, relatively rare two-light version with subtle upsweep where front wing meets rear wing.*

Silver Dawn: *Park Ward drophead coupe, interior view showing folding rear seat and optional fitted luggage.*

Silver Dawn: Park Ward drophead coupe, four-light version with the more common wing treatment.

Silver Dawn: *Hooper saloon in an early version of the "Empress style."*

Silver Dawn: *James Young saloon.*

Silver Dawn: *Henri Chapron drop-head coupe.*

Silver Cloud I and SI

1955-1959

6

With the introduction in April 1955 of the S series cars (which would in time become known as the SI series) the death knell was sounded in earnest for the coachbuilding trade. For here was a car so lovely of line that the coachbuilders were hard pressed to improve upon it, and this at a price substantially less than a custom bodied car. This model was lower and wider than its predecessors and featured a chassis which had 50% more torsional rigidity than the SD/Mk.VI/R-type. This was the last series to utilize the six cylinder engine, and for the first time a production Rolls-Royce was equiped with dual carburetors. This made Rolls-Royce and Bentley exactly the same for the first time since Bentley was acquired by the Company.

The popular automatic transmission was now a standard fitting and the loss of the manual gearbox seemed to be of small consequence to most. Gone too was the lovely sunshine roof as a standard item. This was eliminated for the sake of a stronger body shell, although non-stressed panels such as doors, bonnet and boot lid were still made of aluminum as a weight saving measure. The new interior was convenient as well as spacious, and the boot offered generous luggage accommodations. The new chassis provided a feeling of comfort and security and was above all, silent. Ride control was retained but the infinitely adjustable control found on the earlier cars was superseded by a two-position switch mounted on the side of the steering column. The centralised chassis lubrication system also remained, controlled by a foot pump under the dashboard and a fluid reservoir mounted on the firewall in the engine compartment. This system, which had been used by Rolls-Royce for many years, lubricates the entire chassis and suspension through a series of small tubes and drip fittings, by simply depressing the foot pedal under the dash. This should be done about every 100 miles when on the highways or at the beginning of each day's driving when staying in town. If the system is working as it should the pedal will return slowly when depressed; if it pops back up immediately it should be looked into further. The braking system was hydraulic front and rear for the first time, and this was upgraded in April of 1956 by the addition of a second master cylinder and brake fluid reservoir. October, 1956 saw power steering become a fitting.

The S series proved to be one of the most popular as well as financially successful models yet produced, and export sales soared. An advertising campaign which altered the American public's conception of a Rolls-Royce

Investment Rating: RR 6, B 5

from that of a formal, chauffeur-driven vehicle, to a car for more casual personal use was largely responsible. In 1957 while riding the crest of the Company's great sales success, a long wheelbase version was offered. Aimed at the customer requiring a dual-purpose vehicle, this was a model nearly as practical for family use as the standard saloon, yet capable of being pressed onto service for traditional formal purposes when required. Park Ward created these cars by stretching the standard model four inches to a wheelbase of 127″, thereby giving the needed room for a division. This work was beautifully carried out and the division was finished in Circassian Walnut to match the rest of the interior woodwork. Incorporated into the division panel were not only the buttons to raise or lower the glass, but controls for fresh air and heating, a cigar lighter, and a radio speaker box with volume knob for the rear passengers. The speaker boxes were finished in either wood or covered in leather. Most LWB models had fitted into the rear center armrest, leather covered vanities embossed with the R-R crest. These consisted of a ladies compact, a cigarette case, and a note pad and pencil. Occasionally these vanities were fitted into standard wheelbase models as well. The LWB conversion included the addition of opening quarter lights (windows), which were fitted aft of the rear doors in the rear roof pillars, thus making the car a six-light saloon. Of the 156 Rolls-Royce and Bentley LWB models produced in this series, it is believed that less than a dozen were delivered without a division, but with or without the division these long wheelbase versions are generally considered among the more desirable of the production S series cars.

The series continued to be upgraded and in 1957 on U.S. and Canadian exports and 1958 on home market models, the compression was raised from 6.6:1 to 8:1 and the carburetors were enlarged from 1¾″ to 2″, giving the final increase in power to the venerable six cylinder, but this was its swan song as the era of the V8 had arrived and all cars produced by Rolls-Royce henceforth would utilize this engine.

Bentley S1: *standard steel saloon.*

ENGINE

Type: F-head inline six cylinder

Bore & stroke, displacement: 3¾″ × 4½″, 4887cc

Compression ratio: 6.6:1; 1957 8:1 U.S. export models; 1958 8:1 all models

Carburetion: Twin 1¾″ S.U.s; 1958 twin 2″ S.U.s

CHASSIS AND DRIVETRAIN

Transmission: 4-speed automatic, ratios 3.82:1, 2.63:1, 1.45:1, 1:1

Final drive: 3.42:1

Suspension: Front, independent, unequal length wishbones with coil springs and hydraulic dampers; Rear, semi-elliptic springs with controllable hydraulic dampers, Z-type anti-roll bar.

Steering: Cam and roller, 1956 power steering optional

Brakes: Front, self-adjusting hydraulic; Rear, combined hydraulic and mechanical. Mechanical servo assist

GENERAL

Wheelbase:	Std. 123″; LWB 127″
Track: Front:	58″
Rear:	60″
Tires:	8.20 × 15″
Weight:	Std. approx. 4400 lbs.
Number produced:	R-R std. 2238, LWB 121; B std. 3072, LWB 35

Silver Cloud: *standard steel saloon. Placement of clock in center of instrument cluster helps identify this as a Silver Cloud I.*

Silver Cloud I: *James Young long wheelbase saloon.*

Silver Cloud I: *interior view, long wheelbase saloon (Park Ward conversion).*

Silver Cloud I: *Hooper long wheelbase saloon.*

S1: *Freestone and Webb saloon.*

S1: *Freestone and Webb saloon.*

Bentley S1: *H.J. Mulliner drophead coupe, design number 7409. This is the four-light version.*

Silver Cloud I: *H.J. Mulliner drophead coupe. Two-light version, the more commonly seen four-light configuration bore design number 7410.*

S1: H.J. Mulliner Lightweight saloon shown with its owner Dr. Sam Shoup, first president of the Rolls-Royce Owners Club.

Bentley S1: *James Young two-door saloon. Note interesting treatment of head and fog lights.*

Silver Cloud I: *James Young sedanca coupe, design number SC 23.*

SILVER CLOUD II AND S2

1959-1962

7

At the London Motor Show in October 1959, a bold step was taken by conservative Rolls-Royce Limited: the displaying of the new all-aluminum V8 engine. Until this time it had been Company policy not to display engines at motor shows. The Company has never been known to rush the development of any product change, and a V8 had been in the planning stages as far back as 1947. As early as 1954, development of the new engine was sufficiently advanced that a prototype had run on a test bed by the end of that year.

The need for increased performance was clearly evident from the competitive pressure of other luxury cars on the market. Rolls-Royce had the 5675cc inline eight cylinder that had been used in the Phantom IV, but its length made the thought of using it in a modern production car unacceptable. A Vee configuration was the logical step, and the Company had had plenty of experience with this engine design. Before the war they had produced the great Merlin V12 aero engines as well as the aluminum V12 which was used in the Phantom III.

The all aluminum construction of the new power unit allowed them to achieve their goal of "no weight increase." This coupled with approximately 30% more horsepower made for startling performance in this large automobile. Acceleration from 0 to 60 could be

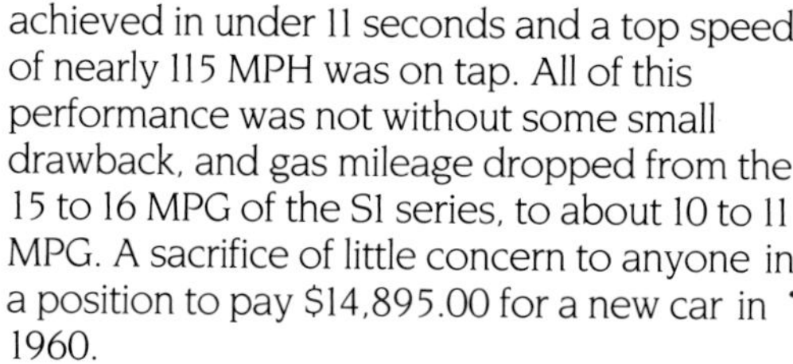

achieved in under 11 seconds and a top speed of nearly 115 MPH was on tap. All of this performance was not without some small drawback, and gas mileage dropped from the 15 to 16 MPG of the S1 series, to about 10 to 11 MPG. A sacrifice of little concern to anyone in a position to pay $14,895.00 for a new car in 1960.

The outward appearance of the series 2 cars was virtually unchanged from the first series, making quick identification difficult, but a glance inside will tell the difference. The series 2 cars have louvered air outlets on the facia caprail, and the clock, which on the earlier series cars was incorporated into the cluster of minor gauges, now lived by itself next to the speedometer, which incidentally, now read to 120 MPH. Cruising speed was increased by raising the rear axle ratio commensurate with the increase in power.

The car remained whisper quiet, as always, due in part to the fact that the body had no metal-to-metal contact with the chassis except through the speedometer cable. A new system of chassis lubrication utilized 21 grease-gun fittings and required servicing only at 10,000 mile intervals. This replaced the time honored one-shot, pedal pump system that had served for so many years.

Investment Rating: RR 5, B 4

Bentley ***S2:*** *standard steel saloon.*

Some of the early V8s had valve guide problems, but many of these cars, particularly in the U.S., went back to dealers for correction of this trouble. The problem manifests itself as smoking and excessive oil consumption. This occurred in the early cars because valve stem seals were not used at that time. The situation can be corrected by removing and machining the heads to fit the new-type valve guides which utilize the seals. At the same time it is wise to replace the early-style metal head-gaskets, which have proven troublesome, with the later composition type. A number of design modifications took place after the start of the SXC series of Rolls-Royce and the CU series of Bentley. These changes encompassed the starter, valve guides, cam and lifters, and also the rocker arms and shafts.

Minor updates during the series included the addition of a rear radio speaker with balance control in October 1960, while in October of 1961 sliding doors were fitted to the front door cubby holes and the instrument lighting was changed to blue. The one update which many lamented, came about in August 1962 when the headlights were changed to the sealed-beam variety, replacing the lovely lights which had borne the intertwined RR or the Bentley B monogram on their centers in previous years.

ENGINE

Type: Overhead valve V8

Bore & stroke, displacement: 4.1″ × 3.6″, 6230cc

Compression ratio: 8:1

Carburetion: Twin HD6 1¾″ S.U.s

CHASSIS AND DRIVETRAIN

Transmission: 4-speed automatic, ratios 3.82:1, 2.63:1, 1.45:1, 1:1

Final drive: 3.08:1

Suspension: Front, independent, unequal length wishbones with coil springs, hydraulic dampers and anti-roll bar; Rear, semi-elliptic springs, controllable hydraulic dampers, single radius rod

Steering: Power assisted cam and roller

Brakes: Front, self-adjusting hydraulic; Rear, combined hydraulic and mechanical; mechanical servo assist, finned drums

GENERAL

Wheelbase: .... Std. 123″; LWB 127″

Track: Front: .... 58½″

Rear: .... 60″

Tires: .... 8.20 × 15″

Weight: .... Std. approx. 4560 lbs.

Number produced: .... R-R std. 2417, LWB 299; B std. 1865, LWB 57

***Silver Cloud II:** long wheelbase saloon with division.*

***Bentley S2:** the new V8 chassis as introduced for Rolls-Royce and Bentley in 1959.*

***View of the H.J. Mulliner coachbuilding factory** showing a Silver Cloud II drophead coupe and Bentley S2 Continentals.*

Bentley S2: *drophead coupe. The popular conversion carried out by H.J. Mulliner on Bentley and Rolls-Royce chassis from standard steel components.*

Silver Cloud II: *long wheelbase saloon by Hooper. This car which was exhibited at the 1959 London Motor Show marked the end of Hooper's production.*

Silver Cloud II: *James Young long wheelbase saloon with division to design number SCT100.*

Silver Cloud III and S3

1962-1966

8

The Silver Cloud III and Bentley S3 were the final configuration of the very popular S series of cars. They used the same basic body shell as the S1 and S2 series but with a considerable number of changes and refinements, the most obvious of which was the fitting of four headlamps and a lower radiator shell which produced a slightly sloping bonnet line and somewhat lower frontal appearance. The front wings were more sharply arched, and the marker lights were taken from the top of the wings and moved forward and down. The bumpers now featured smaller overriders, although most of the coachbuilt and U.S. delivery models still used the large, older style. The interior too was changed with a padded caprail above the facia and separate seats in the front. Two inches additional leg room was provided in the rear, and rear seating space was widened in January 1964. Two inch carburetors and increasing the compression ratio to 9:1, along with a new distributor incorporating a vacuum advance mechanism, resulted in 7% more horsepower. This boost in power brought the maximum speed up to nearly 120 mph.

Rolls-Royce was at this time, anxious to broaden its field of potential buyers and to demonstrate that the cars emanating from this firm could be ". . . driven in a truly sporting manner as a young man's car." To prove this point the Company enlisted Grand Prix driver Tony Brooks to evaluate a standard Silver Cloud III during a grueling three-part test. The first portion of the test was high speed motoring at the 2.4 mile Goodwood racing circuit, during which, under wet and rainy conditions, Mr. Brooks found the car "extremely light to handle in relation to its size. . . " and was ". . . very surprised at its controlability . . . . there was no tendency to oversteer or understeer." When the track dried brake tests were conducted with three passengers on board. The brakes proved excellent, with eight consecutive stops being made from speeds of 90 to 100 mph. The brakes were said to show "only a very slight tendency to fade . . . . but otherwise they were first class." The next stage was conducted in France where Brooks, accompanied by his wife and another couple covered 739 miles in one day, leaving Mr. Brooks to comment, "I can honestly say that I'm good for many more miles of motoring yet. I've never arrived at the end of a similiar journey less tired." The final stage was a torturous drive over a mountain circuit in the Alpes Maritimes, full of hairpin turns and steep descents. At the end of two weeks and 2,700 miles Tony Brooks summed up by saying, "the pleasure that I found in driving the Silver Cloud came from a balance of qualities that is unique in my experience. The result is that the car gives you high performance motoring as near effortless as it can be under all the varied road

Investment Rating: RR 7, B 6

*S**ilver Cloud III:** long wheelbase saloon.*

conditions experienced on test . . . . . there is nothing quite like it." The point was made.

Production of the Silver Clouds was drawing to an end with the introduction of the all new monocoque construction Silver Shadow in October 1965. Yet there was still demand for a Rolls-Royce, other than a Phantom, with a separate chassis, upon which specialty coachwork could be built. So in late 1965 and until March 1966, with the Silver Shadow already in production, two special series of Silver Cloud chassis were produced. These were the CSC series, which stood for Coachbuilt Silver Cloud, running from CSC1B to CSC141B and CSC1C to CSC19C for a total of 79 cars, odd numbers only being used and the number 13 omitted.

The Silver Cloud III and S3 were probably the best of the entire Silver Cloud series, owing to the many updates and constant refinement which took place throughout the years in which these cars were produced. They are powerful and are as nice to drive today as they were nearly 20 years ago when the last of the series left the factory. As to the aesthetics of four headlight S3s versus the two of the S1 and S2 series, it is purely a matter of personal preference, and will no doubt be debated as long as Rolls-Royce enthusiasts gather together.

ENGINE
Type: Overhead valve V8
Bore & stroke, displacement: 4.1″ × 3.6″, 6230cc
Compression ratio: 9:1 or 8:1 available
Carburetion: Twin HD8 2″ S.U.s

CHASSIS AND DRIVETRAIN
Transmission: 4-speed automatic, ratios 3.82:1, 2.63:1, 1.45:1, 1:1
Final drive: 3.08:1
Suspension: Front, independent, unequal length wishbones with coil springs, hydraulic dampers and anti-roll bar; Rear, semi-elliptic springs, controllable hydraulic dampers, single radius rod
Steering: Power assisted cam and roller
Brakes: Front, self-adjusting hydraulic; Rear, combined hydraulic and mechanical; mechanical servo assist, finned drums, two separate hydraulic systems and master cylinders

GENERAL
Wheelbase: .... Std. 123″; LWB 127″
Track: Front: .... 58½″
Rear: .... 60″
Tires: .... 8.20 × 15″
Weight: .... Std. approx. 4560 lbs.
Number produced: .... R-R std. 2445, LWB 253, CSC 79; B std. 1286, LWB 32

Bentley S3: standard steel saloon.

Silver Cloud III: drophead coupe, H.J. Mulliner conversion to design number 7504.

Silver Cloud III: this James Young six-light saloon is often erroneously referred to as a Flying Spur, a name reserved for H.J. Mulliner's design which appeared on Bentley S series Continentals and a few late Silver Cloud IIIs.

Silver Cloud III: *James Young two-door saloon on a late CSC series chassis.*

Silver Cloud III: *H.J. Mulliner Flying Spur sports saloon.*

Silver Cloud III: *Park Ward fixedhead coupe.*

Silver Shadow and T-Type

1966-1977

9

The introduction of any new model from Rolls-Royce is always an event and therefore well covered in the press. But the unveiling of the Silver Shadow and T-type Bentley was to cause a stir in the motoring journals the like of which had never been seen before with the introduction of a new car from this conservative company. The Silver Shadow was the end product of ten years research and development and represented the most radically new car to emerge from the works since the Silver Ghost. The only thing that this car had in common with its predecessors was the basic V-8 engine, and even this had been fitted with redesigned cylinder heads featuring improved combustion chambers and repositioned spark plugs. The new car was 6¾″ shorter, 4½″ lower, and 3¾″ narrower than the Silver Cloud III, yet offered nearly the same interior room in a far more efficient package. Gone was the classic, flowing body style which had been for so long associated with Rolls-Royce.

But in its place was a car truly engineered for the Seventies. It was of monocoque construction and used a stressed steel body shell with galvanized steel in the underbody assembly for resistance to rust. The doors, bonnet, and boot lid were again made of aluminum in the interest of saving weight. To this monocoque structure were fitted front and rear subframes which carried the engine and suspension. The suspension was independent at all four wheels, and disc brakes were fitted fore and aft. The brakes utilized three separate hydraulic circuits, two of which were incorporated into the automatic, hydraulic height control system. The 11″ brake discs used two separate calipers on the front, and a single dual caliper on the rear. The hydraulic system which powered the brakes, as well as the automatic height control, was driven by pumps which ran off of the engine and supplied hydraulic pressure to two accumulators which operated at 2500 lbs. per square inch. Of these two units, the forward accumulator actuated the front caliper on the front wheels and half of the caliper on the rear wheels. The rearward accumulator actuated the rear caliper on the front wheels and the automatic height control. The remaining portions of the rear wheel calipers was operated by a conventional master cylinder actuated by foot pedal pressure. With this system it would be possible to lose one or even two circuits and not be without brakes. It is important to note here that this is a potential trouble area, and when considering the purchase of an older Shadow it is wise to have it inspected by an authorized dealer to insure that there is no fluid leakage and that this rather complex system is working as it should. U.S. delivery cars featured an all new three speed automatic transmission with torque converter, while home market cars used an

Investment Rating: 6

improved version of the old four speed automatic until July 1968. The price of the new car had increased to over $19,000 in the U.S., but this now included air conditioning as a standard feature on American delivery cars. It would be November 1969 before air conditioning became standard on all cars.

By this time all of the major coachbuilders were gone, with the exception of James Young and, of course, the company's own Mulliner-Park Ward. James Young modified 43 Rolls-Royce and 7 Bentleys into two door saloons before their coachbuilding activities were ended in 1967. Mulliner-Park Ward also offered a two door saloon version of the Shadow which they introduced in March of 1966. In September of the following year they brought out a convertible version as well. These two offerings were to become the Corniche in 1971.

Between its introduction in October 1965 and its being replaced by the Silver Shadow II in 1977, the Shadow was the object of constant upgrading and refinement. Here then, listed in chronological order, are some of the more noteworthy changes:

1968 saw the front seat backs widened and more heavily padded, but the newly enacted U.S. Federal Safety Standards put an end to the lovely wood veneer picnic trays for the rear seat passengers. These same standards required that the mascot be spring loaded which resulted in the first 400 USA cars coming over without mascots; spring loaded flying ladies were supplied later. In mid 1969 a long wheelbase model was introduced. It could be had either with or without a division window and was in fact one of the first production cars to be federalized in the U.S. with a division. In the interest of safety the division was no longer finished in the beautiful walnut veneers as in years past, but was now finished in padded leather. The long wheelbase model had separate air conditioning units front and rear and sported a dual radio installation as well. Side marker lights were fitted, and the interior redesigned to incorporate flush mounted door handles and other safety features. In early 1968 at about chassis number 6500 the steering ratio was increased to 19.3:1, which resulted in only 3½ turns being required from lock to lock.

In early 1970, at chassis #9000, reflectors were incorporated into the side markers, while engine displacement was enlarged from 6230cc to 6750cc and the compression ratio reduced to 8:1. Also at chassis #9000, centralised door locking was fitted, along with a remote controlled exterior mirror. Stereo tape became an option. In mid 1971 steering was once again modified this time to a ratio of 17.5:1 for 3.2 turns lock to lock and cruise control, which would become standard with the A series cars in 1972, was offered as an option. From August 1972 on, compliant front suspension was used along with the fitting of 205×15 radial ply tires and after chassis #13754, a complete electrical package change took place which included the boot lid in the operation of the central locking system. Mid 1973 ventilated discs were fitted to the front brakes. Later in 1973 in the 16000 chassis series we saw what was to become known as the '73½ model. This included deleting the air intakes below the headlights and the fitting of energy absorbing bumpers front and rear (rubber bumpers) while slotted wheel covers came slightly later.

In early 1974, at chassis #18269, minor suspension changes took place, and the wheel arches were enlarged to accommodate HR70×15 wide profile tires. Late 1974 saw compression reduced to 7.3:1 for U.S. and Canadian models, and a different type of coil and ballast resistor, along with Lucas OPUS electronic ignition, became standard equipment. Late 1975, at about chassis #22000, the triplicate braking system was changed to dual with the deletion of the master cylinder. The modifications listed above detail only some of the many changes which have taken place over the years and pertain mainly to U.S. delivery cars. Specifications can differ for home market and foreign delivery models.

This process of constant refinement, combined with such procedures as weighing, matching and balancing of all critical engine parts, and the use of only the finest quality components available, results in an engine that

***Silver Shadow:** standard saloon.*

***Bentley T-type:** standard saloon.*

Silver Shadow: long wheelbase saloon.

ENGINE

Type: Overhead valve V8

Bore & stroke, displacement: 4.1″×3.6″, 6230cc; 1970 4.1″×3.9″, 6750cc

Compression ratio: 9:1; 1970 reduced to 8:1; 1975 reduced to 7.3:1 U.S. version

Carburetion: Twin HD8 S.U.s

CHASSIS AND DRIVETRAIN

Transmission: 4-speed automatic, ratios 3.82:1, 2.63:1, 1.45:1, 1:1; U.S. version, 3-speed with torque converter, ratios 2.48:1, 1.48:1, 1:1, becoming std. all models Nov. 1968

Final drive: 3.08:1

Suspension: Front, independent, coil springs, double wishbones, telescopic hydraulic dampers; Rear, independent coil spring by trailing arms, telescopic hydraulic dampers, automatic height control operated by engine driven hydraulic pump

Steering: Power assisted recirculating ball

Brakes: Front and rear, power assisted 11″ discs, triplicate hydraulic system, changed to duplicate system 1975, ventilated front discs mid 1973

GENERAL

Wheelbase: .... Std. 119½″; LWB 123½″

Track: Front: .... 57½″

Rear: .... 57½″

Tires: ... 8.45×15″, 1972 205×15″, 1974 HR 70×15″

Weight: .... Std. approx. 4650 lbs.

Number produced: .... N/A

Silver Shadow: long wheelbase saloon with division, interior view. Safety regulations have brought about deletion of much of the lovely woodwork as used in the past.

Silver Shadow: H.J. Mulliner-Park Ward fixedhead coupe.

is without equal. In the course of production one out of each one hundred engines is selected at random and bench run for eight hours. It is then completely disassembled and tolerances are checked against factory specifications. Every single engine is bench run for the equivalent of one hundred fifty miles, then installed in the car and subjected to two further thirty mile driving tests. This attention to detail is carried out in order to assure that the finished automobile is as near perfection as is humanly possible.

In summary the Silver Shadow is a very different automobile than any of the Rolls-Royce models which came before it. While its highly sophisticated technology placed it in a class by itself for ride, silence and luxury this same complexity makes for higher maintenance requirements to assure that all systems remain functioning as intended.

Bentley T-type: *James Young produced 50 of these rather awkward fixed-head coupes on early Silver Shadow and T-type chassis. Compare this to the more graceful design by H.J. Mulliner-Park Ward.*

Silver Shadow: *H.J. Mulliner-Park Ward drophead coupe.*

Corniche

1971-PRESENT

10

The name "Corniche" comes from a stretch of coastline in the south of France between Nice and Italy. This area was often the destination for cross-continental travelers on holiday. It was considered a proper test of an automobile to make this Grand Tour and to arrive in comfort and style. Therefore, it was fitting to use the name "Corniche" on a sleek Grand Touring motor car, and this is exactly what Rolls-Royce did with the prototype Mark V Bentley shortly before the second world war broke out. This original Corniche featured independent front suspension and had an aerodynamic body produced by Van Vooren of Paris. While nearing completion of a 15,000 mile endurance test on the continent the prototype was seriously damaged in a road accident. The car was dismantled and the chassis shipped back to England for repairs while the body was attended to by a French coachbuilding firm. When the body was repaired it was taken to the docks for shipment to England and while awaiting a ship was destroyed in a bombing raid as war began.

It was this name that was revived and given to the H.J. Mulliner-Park Ward two-door saloons and convertibles in 1971. These cars could be purchased either as a Rolls-Royce or Bentley, and were the same body style which had been being marketed since 1966 and 1967 respectively, as coachbuilt variations of the

standard saloons. The intent was to give these cars improved performance and an individual identity. A 10% increase in power was effected by changes to ignition and valve timing, a more efficient air cleaner and a 2½″ dual exhaust system. It was the first Rolls-Royce model to be fitted with radial tires as standard equipment. The 205×15″ tires first used were later replaced by HR70×15″ or 235×15″ wide profile rubber. Earlier Corniche models featured a 15″ diameter wood rimmed steering wheel, which was later changed for a 16″ wheel made of plastic and finally to the leather rimmed wheel which is used presently. The facia was redesigned and carried a full set of instruments which included a tachometer, while the radiator shell of the Corniche was nearly half an inch deeper than the Silver Shadow. At a quick outward glance one could recognize this new car by the special wheel-covers which were designed for use on the Corniche alone.

The exterior appearance of the Corniche was altered, along with that of the Silver Shadow, in mid 1973 by the addition of rubber bumpers and the accompanying changes which occurred at that time. Rather than list all of the changes that have taken place since the introduction of this car, the reader will be referred to the chapters on the Silver Shadow, Silver Shadow II and the Silver Spirit, since virtually all of the updates incorporated into those models apply equally to the Corniche.

Investment Rating: 8

*R**olls-Royce Corniche:** saloon, the company's new name for the H.J. Mulliner-Park Ward fixedhead coupe.*

The one major exception to this was the suspension. In 1974 work was started on a redesigned and improved rear suspension system. The three prime objectives were: to achieve better handling, to reduce road noise and to improve ride comfort. The new design was developed over a period of four years, and in 1979 it was fitted to the Corniche and the Camargue. Its use on the four door models however, was held over until the introduction of the Silver Spirit in October of 1980.

The steel body shells for the Corniche are manufactured by Mulliner-Park Ward then fitted with the engine and drivetrain at the Rolls-Royce factory at Crewe. These units are then returned to Mulliner-Park Ward in London for completion. Each car takes approximately four months to build. All procedures are done by hand in the centuries-old manner of coach-building. One example of the myriad of steps to completion is the process involved in building the folding top for the convertible. It takes one man four days to build the frame-work alone for this top, using a complex master jig, next one week is spent making the fully headlined, padded top, which when erected, is nearly indistinguishable from a fixed roof. It is this level of craftsmanship combined with the technical sophistication of this car that make it a "Gran Turismo" in the purest sense of the word.

ENGINE
Type: Overhead valve V8
Bore & stroke, displacement: 4.1″ × 3.9″, 6750cc
Compression ratio: 9:1, 1972 8:1 U.S. version, 1973 7.3:1 U.S. version
Carburetion: Twin HD8 S.U.s, 1977 twin HIF7 S.U.s

CHASSIS AND DRIVETRAIN
Transmission: 3-speed with torque converter, ratios 2.48:1, 1.48:1, 1:1
Final drive: 3.08:1
Suspension: Front, independent, coil springs, double wishbones, telescopic hydraulic dampers; Rear, independent coil spring by trailing arms, telescopic hydraulic dampers, automatic height control operated by engine driven hydraulic pump; 1977 raised upper suspension arm joints
Steering: Power assisted recirculating ball, 1977 rack and pinion
Brakes: Front and rear, power assisted 11″ discs, triplicate hydraulic system, changed to duplicate system 1975, ventilated front discs mid 1973

GENERAL
Wheelbase: .... 119½″, 1977 120″
Track: Front: .... 57½″, 1977 60″
Rear: .... 57½″, 1977 60½″
Tires: .... 205 × 15″, 1974 HR70 × 15″
Weight: .... Approx. 5200 lbs.
Number produced: .... N/A

***Rolls-Royce Corniche:** convertible (Company's terminology). New wheel-covers and trim badges on the boot lid gave the new Corniche, with its more potent engine a separate identity.*

***Bentley Corniche:** saloon.*

Bentley Corniche: *a late model convertible, contemporary with the Silver Spirit. The saloon is no longer offered. This European-delivery model is fitted with the front air dam and headlight washer/wipers.*

CAMARGUE

1975-PRESENT

II

Camargue (pronounced Ka-marg) is, to quote from an introductory piece from the Company, "a wild watery area in the South of France, described by the Michelin Guide as one of the strangest, most solitary, most original regions of France. It is home to a special breed of half-wild white horses which has flourished in the Camargue since Roman times; like filmy white wraiths, never to be tamed." This conjures up romantic images and quickens the pulse which is exactly what Rolls-Royce wanted for this, their ultimate personal luxury car. The inspiration for the Camargue was a special one-off design exercise on a Bentley T-type by Sergio Pininfarina for the 1968 Paris Salon and Earl's Court Motor Show. Many hoped that this car would be the fore-runner to a new Bentley Continental model. It is mouth-watering indeed to think of this car in production and fitted with the turbo charging system of today's Mulsaune Turbo, but alas this was not to be. Bentley was not as well known nor as well received in the U.S. as Rolls-Royce, this along with other considerations influenced the decision to develop the car as a Rolls-Royce.

In March 1975, after a gestation period of nearly 7 years, the Camargue was born. The body had been somewhat changed by Pininfarina from his original design on the Bentley but it was easy to see who had fathered this car. The production bodies, made of steel with

the usual aluminum doors, bonnet and boot lid, were built by Mulliner-Park Ward, the Rolls-Royce coachbuilders. While the Camargue shared the same overall dimension of 207½ inches with the Corniche, it was ¾″ lower and 3½″ wider. Interior room had been increased 8½″ in the rear seat and the boot had gained 3 cubic feet of carrying capacity. The seats were upholstered in Nuella hides which are vat dyed and will not show scuffs, since the color is all through the leather, not merely on the surface. Wilton wool carpet edged in the same leather was used and Circassian Walnut veneers applied to the facia and garnish rails. The steering wheel was trimmed in leather.

As in the Silver Shadow, standard equipment included electrically operated gear selection, windows, radio antenna, gasoline filler door, windshield wipers and washers, rear window demister and centralized door locking system. AM-FM radio and Quadraphonic tape player were also included in the standard fittings. Two of its new features that have since been incorporated into all new models are the ice-warning system, which alerts the driver to possible icy road conditions, and Lucas OPUS electronic ignition. The major engineering innovation on this car was the very sophisticated automatic air conditioning system which offered independent temperature control at

Investment Rating: 8

Camargue: as offered at introduction.

two levels. This allowed the occupants to have air of one temperature for upper body and face while maintaining a different setting for lower body and feet. Once set, electronic sensors would maintain constant temperature, summer or winter.

Mechanical specifications are virtually the same as on the Silver Shadow and Corniche. As in keeping with past company policy, horsepower figures are not quoted. A Solex four-barrel carburetor is used except in the U.S. and Japan where twin S.U.s are standard. A dual exhaust system is used, again excepting those models equipped for export as above. U.S. cars receive a single exhaust with a catalytic converter, while those bound for Japan are fitted with the conventional Silver Shadow arrangement.

The Camargue was envisioned as a very limited production car and this it remains. For with all of its refinement and exotic Italian designed coachwork the Camargue has never achieved wide popularity.

ENGINE
Type: Overhead valve V8
Bore & stroke, displacement: 4.1″ × 3.9″, 6750cc
Compression ratio: 8:1, U.S. version 7.3:1
Carburetion: Solex four choke, U.S. twin HD8 S.U.s, 1977 twin HIF7 S.U.s

CHASSIS AND DRIVETRAIN
Transmission: 3-speed with torque converter, ratios 2.48:1, 1.48:1, 1:1
Final drive: 3.08:1
Suspension: Front, independent, coil springs, double wishbones, telescopic hydraulic dampers; Rear, independent coil spring by trailing arms, telescopic hydraulic dampers, automatic height control operated by engine driven hydraulic pump; front and rear anti-roll bars
Steering: Power assisted recirculating ball, 1977 rack and pinion
Brakes: Four wheel power assisted 11″ discs, ventilated front discs

GENERAL
Wheelbase: .... 120½″
Track: Front: .... 60″
Rear: .... 60½″
Tires: .... HR70 × 15″
Weight: .... 5135 lbs.
Number produced: .... N/A

Bentley T-type: *Pininfarina's special show prototype for 1968. It was hoped that this car would be the forerunner of a new Bentley Continental but turned out in fact to be the inspiration for the Camargue.*

Camargue: *late model, contemporary with Silver Spirit. Plated trim strip below window sill has been deleted in favor of pinstriping running the length of the body. Note the addition of a wiper for each headlight.*

SILVER SHADOW II AND T2 1977-1980

12

Despite the objections of those who, upon its introduction, decried the Silver Shadow as "no longer looking like a Rolls-Royce," the model went on to be a smashing success. By February 1977, when the Silver Shadow II and Bentley T2 were released, the car had been in production for nearly twelve years. At this time an all new car was rumored to be in the works; nonetheless the Silver Shadow received major redesigning and was renamed the Silver Shadow II.

The interior retained the traditional wood and leather but the instrument layout was completely revised. An electronic speedometer replaced the previous cable driven instrument and eliminated the last possibility of noise coming from the facia. It featured a pushbutton trip reset and an odometer which read to 999,999, a statement of self-assurance in keeping with the quality and longevity of the marque. A four-in-one gauge arrangement was mounted next to the speedometer and kept tabs on fuel level, oil pressure, amps and coolant temperature. A light panel warned of low pressure in the hydraulic systems, brake fluid level, stoplight failure, parking brake release and engine overheating, as well as low coolant, washer fluid level, low fuel and icy road conditions. A thermometer in the facia shows outside ambient air temperature and there is of course, an electric clock. Switches for the speed control now located on the gear change stalk permitted set speed to be advanced without using the accelerator pedal. Steering wheel diameter was reduced to 15½″ in the interest of better instrument visibility and comfort.

The superb dual level air conditioning system from the Camargue was adopted. This system draws air from outside of the car, then dehumidifies and cools it to 32 degrees Fahrenheit. The air is then brought up to the temperature which has been selected—between 63° F and 91° F—and enters the interior through either the upper or lower set of ducts. The dual level controls, which operate independently, allow one to have a cool face and warm feet or vice versa. Exterior changes included the fitting of U.S. style bumpers to cars in all markets, a new name plate on the boot lid, modified door handles, and a radiator shell which was .47″ taller, but it was the mechanical changes that were the big news. New power-assisted rack and pinion steering replaced the recirculating ball unit previously used, a modification which greatly increased precision and driver "feel." Handling was improved by raising the upper suspension arms and by use of a redesigned anti-sway bar, thus keeping the front wheels more upright in a hard cornering situation for increased

Investment Rating: 7

Silver Shadow II: standard saloon.

stability, while reducing tire wear. The HD8 S.U. carburetors were replaced with the emission efficient, tamper-proof HIF7 type. These were of a smaller throat size, but any power which might have been lost through the reduced diameter was regained by the fitting of the Corniche-type dual exhaust system. It should also be mentioned that an air dam was fitted under the front bumper on home market and European cars. This was not used on U.S. delivery models because it blocked the air flow under the car and caused the catalytic converter—which U.S. emission regulations require—to overheat. Engine cooling efficiency was increased through the use of a larger, seven-bladed fan and by mounting a thermostatically controlled auxiliary fan in front of the radiator.

The name Wraith, which was first used in the late thrities and again in the forties and fifties, was resurrected and the long wheelbase version was christened the Silver Wraith II. This car afforded the buyer the option of a division, while also giving the rear seat passengers a bit more privacy through the use of a smaller rear window than that which was fitted to the standard model. The long wheelbase version can be identified by its leather-like, Everflex covered top with rear quarter badges and Corniche-style wheelcovers.

The Silver Wraith II, as well as the standard wheelbase Silver Shadow II and Bentley T2 are, with their considerable number of updates, truly the finest of the series and merit serious consideration when contemplating the purchase of a late model Silver Shadow.

Silver Wraith II: *this was the company's new name for the long wheelbase saloon.*

Bentley T2: *standard saloon.*

ENGINE
Type: Overhead valve V8
Bore & stroke, displacement: 4.1″×3.9″, 6750cc
Compression ratio: 7.3:1; raised to 9:1 for countries other than USA, Australia & Japan
Carburetion: Twin HIF7 S.U.s

CHASSIS AND DRIVETRAIN
Transmission: 3-speed automatic with torque converter, ratios 2.48:1, 1.48:1, 1:1
Final drive: 3.08:1
Suspension: Front, independent by lower wishbone, stabilized upper levers, coil springs, hydraulic dampers; Rear, independent by trailing arms, coil springs, hydraulic dampers; Front and rear anti-roll bars, automatic ride height control
Steering: Power assisted rack and pinion
Brakes: Four wheel power assisted 11″ discs, front discs ventilated

GENERAL
Wheelbase: . . . . Std. 120.1″, LWB 124.1″
Track: Front: . . . . 60″
Rear: . . . . 59.6″
Tires: . . . . HR70×15″ or 235/70 HR15″
Weight: . . . . Approx. 4700 lbs.
Number produced: . . . . N/A

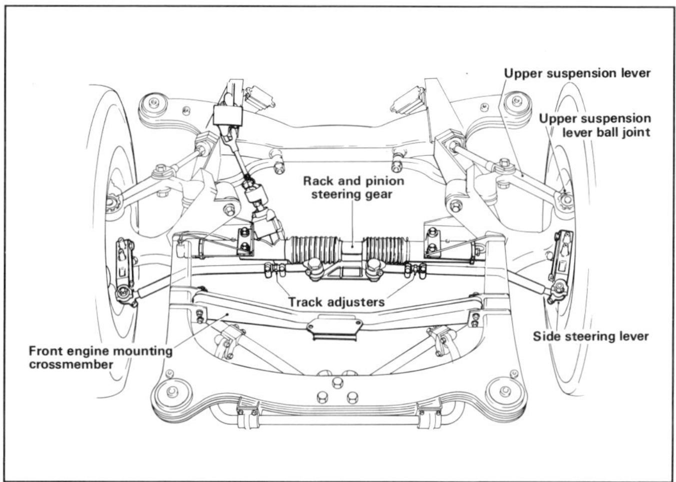

SSII/T2: illustration of new front suspension and rack and pinion steering.

Silver Shadow II: facia and instrument layout.

SS II/T2: rear interior view.

SILVER SPIRIT AND MULSANNE 1980-PRESENT

13

The long awaited new car was announced October 1st, 1980, ending the fifteen year production run of the Silver Shadow. During that time 32,300 cars had been made, 17,000 of which were exported. The new model followed the pattern which had been used in naming its predecessor, Silver Dawn, Silver Cloud, Silver Shadow, and now Silver Spirit, all somehow connoting smoothness and silence. And in keeping with the trend toward more individual identity for the long wheelbase version, it was given a separate name as had been done with the Silver Wraith II. The name chosen, Silver Spur, was derived from the well remembered Bentley Continental Flying Spur, a particularly handsome model offered from the late fifties through the middle sixties. The name Mulsanne, which was given to the new Bentley, was a departure from the practice of using a letter suffix as had been the rule since the introduction of the R-type. The new name made reference to the Mulsanne Straight on the Sarthe Racing Circuit in France, the setting for Bentley's five victories at the twenty four hour LeMans race during the years 1924-1930.

This new series of cars was painstakingly developed over an eight year period. Project Manager, John Astbury stated "for the first time we built twelve pre-production cars so that we could test all our ideas about the design of the car and the best way to build it." This approach resulted in a car which retained traditional Rolls-Royce features and identity while achieving technical advancement and a new "contemporary" look. The look which the stylists wanted would be brought about by reducing apparent height and increasing apparent width. This was achieved by lowering the waistline of the body and using features such as the new wrap-around headlight and tail light assemblies to accentuate horizontal width and length. This effect was further enhanced by the new curved side windows and a 30% increase in total glass area.

The new headlights featured 350,000 candlepower on high-beam and integral washers and wipers. Unfortunately these units are not used on U.S. delivery versions. The tail lights however, are acceptable in all sales markets. The inboard sections of the tail lights are carried on the boot lid and raise with it, thus creating no obstructions when handling luggage. Excellent wet-weather visibility is provided by wipers which sweep a large rectangular area, and rain deflectors fitted at the sides of the windshield which help keep the door windows clear.

The layout of the facia is very much as it was in the Silver Shadow II, but with the addition of a digital display which includes a clock, outside air temperature and resetable

Investment Rating: 7

Silver Spirit: *standard saloon.*

elapsed time reading, which is useful when traveling. New centralized door locking allows the system to be activated by switches on the door cap-rails. Interior detailing still includes vanity mirrors and lights in the rear quarters, and the buyer now has the option of traditional all leather seats or leather with color-keyed textile facings.

Mechanical specifications remain largely unaltered. The well proven 6750cc V8 was given larger main bearings before the introduction of the Silver Spirit and the three-speed torque converter transmission continues to be used. Improvements to the ride and handling were brought about through the use of the redesigned rear suspension which was first used in 1979 on the Corniche and Camargue. The pivots on the semi-trailing arms are now more inclined, causing a greater swing-axle effect and a more pronounced camber change as the wheels rise and fall. This combined with the raised roll center height of the wheels keeps them more upright when cornering and reduces body-roll. Smaller gas-filled springs and struts are now used and have replaced the leveling rams and large springs as were fitted in the past. An additional benefit of these small lighter springs is that they do not intrude into the boot as the older units did.

The entire hydraulic braking and suspension system has been changed to operate on mineral oil rather than the conventional brake fluid which had been employed previously. This provides several benefits. Mineral oil is less corrosive while providing far better lubrication. In addition it has more efficient vibration damping qualities and is non-hygroscopic, which means that it does not absorb water, nor will it encourage water to seep into the

Mulsanne: *standard saloon.*

Silver Spur: *the long wheelbase version of the Silver Spirit.*

hydraulic system. And it is not harmful to paint finish, should it be accidently spilled on body work. All of these things add up to the most sophisticated automobile yet to emerge from the factory at Crewe. Only time will tell if this new model has any chinks in its armor.

ENGINE

Type: Overhead valve V8

Bore & stroke, displacement: 4.1″×3.9″, 6750cc

Compression ratio: 9.0:1

Carburetion: Twin HIF7 S.U.s

CHASSIS AND DRIVETRAIN

Transmission: 3-speed automatic with torque converter, ratios 2.48:1, 1.48:1, 1:1

Final drive: 3.08:1

Suspension: Front, independent by lower wishbone, compliant controlled upper levers, coil springs, telescopic dampers; Rear, independent by semi-trailing arms, suspension struts, gas springs; front and rear anti-roll bars, automatic ride height control

Steering: Power assisted rack and pinion

Brakes: Four wheel power assisted 11″ discs, front discs ventilated

GENERAL

Wheelbase: . . . . Std. 120.5″, LWB 124″

Track: Front: . . . . 60.5″

Rear: . . . . 60.5″

Tires: . . . . 235/70 HR15″

Weight: . . . . Approx. 4950 lbs.

Number produced: . . . . N/A

ROLLS-ROYCE SILVER SPIRIT AND SILVER SPUR REAR SUSPENSION ASSEMBLY

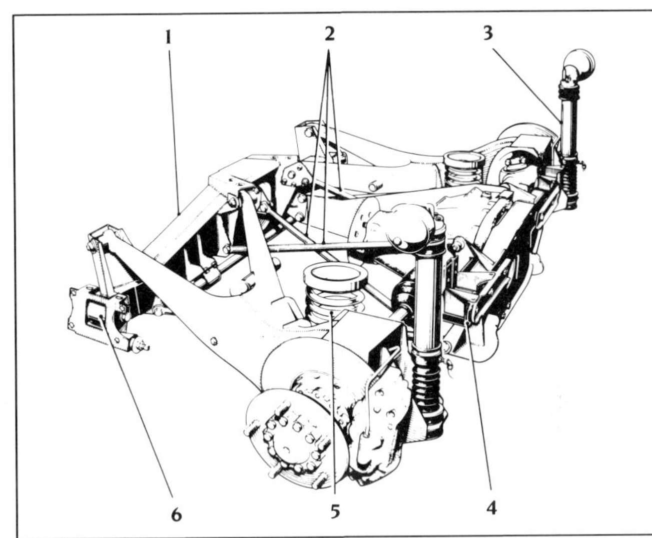

Rear sub-frame, trailing arms, final drive and hub unit

1. Rear crossmember
2. Frame tubes
3. Gas spring and strut
4. Metalastik mount
5. Coil spring
6. Metalastik mount

Silver Spirit: *instrument layout featuring digital display in center of facia.*

MARK VI

1946-1952

14

Even as war clouds gathered over Britain it was realized that continuing to produce complex automobiles, which were largely hand-built and in relatively small numbers, would no longer be economically feasible. Some sort of standardization of manufacturing components had to be brought about if the Company was to go forward in a post-war climate of high taxation and changing social structure.

In the late thirties W.A. Robotham, Rolls-Royce Chief Engineer, said repeatedly that the Company should consider producing its own bodies and that thought should be seriously given to softer springing and even to fitting an automatic transmission. Thus in January 1944, Rolls-Royce began negotiations with the Pressed Steel Company of Oxford who produced nearly all of the steel body panels for the British automobile industry. As a result of these talks, Pressed Steel began making body panels for Rolls-Royce and has continued in that capacity to this day.

The new Bentley had a traditional look about it and was surely influenced by Park Ward's work on the short-lived Bentley Mark V; the Mark VI was an all new car nonetheless. Upon the introduction of this, the first post-war Rolls-Royce automobile, purists decried the engine having been fitted with belts to drive the water pump and generator. These had been gear-driven on the pre-war cars. But it must be remembered that Sir Henry Royce chose to gear drive these components at a time when belts, which were constructed of links pinned together, were not considered reliable. The decision to change to belt drive was done with production costs in mind but only after it had been determined that the new method would be silent and dependable.

Reliability as well as performance were assured by the new F-head engine design. Its robust crankshaft ran in seven copper-lead main bearings and dual S.U. carburetors were fitted. A camshaft was employed which was different from that used in the later, milder, single-carbureted Silver Dawn. Performance was quite remarkable for an automobile which weighed over 4000 lbs. and had the aerodynamic properties of a large breadbox! Acceleration times of 0 to 50 MPH in 12.5 seconds were recorded and a top speed of over 90 MPH was achieved in road tests by contemporary motoring journals. The well known competition driver Mike Couper entered a virtually unmodified Mark VI for the gruelling Monte Carlo Rally in 1949 and was a high overall finisher at the same time winning the Grand Prix de Confort, an award usually reserved for elaborate coachbuilt cars outfitted with every conceivable extra.

In May, 1951 engine displacement was increased from 4¼ litres to 4½ litres and with this came full-flow oil filtration and the more

Investment Rating: 4-6

Mk. VI: standard steel saloon.

efficient dual exhaust system. It is particularly important to change oil frequently in pre "full-flow" cars. Late Mark VIs also saw the fresh-air vent mounted at the top of the scuttle replaced by a ventilator at each side, near the occupants' feet. This greatly increased interior comfort in warm weather.

Rust has been a great problem with the post-war steel bodied cars and the Mark VI, as well as the R-type and Silver Dawn, are certainly no exceptions. Before considering the purchase of any of these models it is essential to examine the body and frame thoroughly for rust and corrosion. Take the car to a nearby service station, raise it on the hoist and look it over completely. Minor surface rust is common to most cars of this era, but beware of cars with severe rust in the body panels and/or the chassis.

The Mark VI has sometimes been referred to as "the beginner's Rolls-Royce." In no way does this demean the car; it simply alludes to the fact that many people have had their introduction to the marque through ownership of one of these cars, your author included. This model has traditionally been the lowest priced

Rolls-Royce product on the collectors' car market, and when one considers that for the price of an ordinary, everyday, new car he can buy a nice Mark VI, this model becomes all the more intriguing.

Mk. VI: *James Young four-door sports saloon. Note earliest type Mk. VI wheelcovers.*

Mk. VI: *Hooper saloon. Variation on the 4-light saloon.*

Mk. VI: *Freestone and Webb's variation of the 6-light semi-razor edged saloon. Interesting comparison with Mulliner's design below.*

ENGINE

Type: F-head inline six cylinder

Bore & stroke, displacement: 3½″×4½″, 4257cc; 1951 3⅝″×4½″, 4566cc

Compression ratio: 6.4:1

Carburetion: Twin 1½″ S.U.s; 1950 twin 1¾″ S.U.s; LHD models stromberg downdraft; 1952 twin S.U.s

CHASSIS AND DRIVETRAIN

Transmission: 4-speed manual, synchro on 2nd, 3rd and 4th, ratios 2.98:1, 2.02:1, 1.34:1, 1:1; 1952 automatic optional, ratios 3.82:1, 2.63:1, 1.45:1, 1:1

Clutch: 10″ long type; 1950 11″ type; 1951 11″ heavy type

Final drive: 3.73:1; 1952 3.41:1 optional

Suspension: Front, independent coil springs, hydraulic dampers; Rear, half-elliptic springs with controllable hydraulic dampers

Steering: Cam and roller, 1950 modified geometry

Brakes: Front, hydraulic; Rear, mechanical. Mechanical servo assist

GENERAL

Wheelbase: . . . . 120″

Track: Front: . . . . 56½″

Rear: . . . . 58⅝″

Tires: . . . . 6.50×16″

Weight: . . . . Approx. 4100 lbs.

Number produced: 5201

Mk. VI: *H.J. Mulliner Lightweight sports saloon.*

Mk. VI: *James Young saloon. Both Park Ward and H.J. Mulliner offered variations of this slab-sided design.*

Mk. VI: *Vanden Plas saloon, One of the few post-war examples from this famous firm.*

*M**k. VI:** James Young two-door sports saloon.*

***Mk. VI:** James Young Saloon Coupe.*

***Mk. VI:** Gurney Nutting sedanca coupe. By this time the famous coachbuilding firm of J. Gurney Nutting had been acquired by Jack Barclay Ltd., who also owned James Young.*

Mk. VI: *fixedhead coupe by Facel Metallon. Note unorthodox radiator treatment.*

Mk. VI: *Freestone and Webb fixedhead coupe.*

Mk. VI: *H.J. Mulliner saloon. This streamline saloon was a forerunner to the Bentley Continental.*

Mk. VI: *Park Ward drophead coupe. One of the rare post-war examples to use side-mounted spare wheels.*

Mk. VI: *Franay drophead coupe. Horns were a later fitting.*

Mk. VI: *Hooper drophead coupe. Open coachwork from this firm on post-war chassis are unusual.*

Mk. VI: *Graber drophead coupe.*

Mk. VI: *Freestone and Webb drophead coupe.*

Mk. VI: *H.J. Mulliner drophead coupe. Note fully disappearing top.*

Mk. VI: *Vanden Plas drophead coupe. another rare post-war body from this coachbuilder.*

R-Type

1952–1955

15

The R-type and long-boot Silver Dawn were more or less interim models as were the Silver Shadow II and Bentley T2 in more recent years. The new model which was to become the S series was being developed, but it would be more than two years before its introduction. So it was felt that by modernizing the Mark VI, now an aging design, the car could remain marketable and would see the Company through until the new model was ready. Thus the R-type was born.

The modernization was accomplished in part by lengthening the frame seven inches behind the rear wheels and elongating the body, achieving a more sleek appearance and increasing luggage capacity. The new design utilized a clamshell type boot lid, replacing the old bottom-hinged arrangement which folded out to make a platform upon which a separate trunk could be carried, as had been the fashion in pre-war days. In addition the less than efficient heating and demisting system was improved with the incorporation of an electrically heated rear window, and the windshield wipers were made more effective by changing to a two-speed motor.

Mechanical components remained much the same aside from an increase in engine compression in 1953. The optional automatic transmission became a standard fitting in lefthand drive cars that same year, and likewise on right drive cars in 1954. The servo-assisted hydraulic front, mechanical rear brake system was continued, as on all post-war models until the introduction of the S series. With the S series the brakes became hydraulic front and rear, although the transmission-driven servo-assist unit was retained. It is not unusual to find on any pre-Silver Shadow/T-type car that the servo is worn or out of adjustment, and the R-type is no exception. This condition is most noticed when coming to rest on an uphill incline, then depressing the brake to hold the car in position. If the servo is not functioning properly, the car may roll back several feet before stopping. This can be prevented by applying the brakes as one approaches the stop and not releasing them until ready to proceed. The problem can be alleviated by relining the servo and/or having it properly adjusted at a knowledgeable service shop. But even when freshly relined and adjusted, "servo lag" can allow the vehicle to move a few inches before the brakes take effect. These observations on the operation of the servo apply to all pre-Silver Shadow models and are not limited to just the R-type. It is therefore wise to test the brakes of any of these cars on an incline before purchase.

The R-type offers a few features not found on the Mark VI, and a slightly more modern body silhouette, but the cars are essentially

Investment Rating: 4-6

R type: standard steel saloon.

the same. Prices for the two models are nearly identical, with condition the primary determining factor, so personal preference will be the major influence when making the choice. Whichever you select, you will be getting a genuine value for your money, assuming price is in line with the market. It should be remembered that it was upon these models that that great thoroughbred, the R-type Continental, was based.

R ***type:*** *Park Ward saloon.*

R type: *Freestone and Webb saloon.*

R type: *H.J. Mulliner Lightweight saloon.*

R type: *Freestone and Webb saloon.*

ENGINE
Type: F-head inline six cylinder
Bore & stroke, displacement: 3⅝″ × 4½″, 4566cc
Compression ratio: 6.4:1, 1953 6.75:1
Carburetion: Twin 1¾″ S.U.s
CHASSIS AND DRIVETRAIN
Transmission: 4-speed manual, synchro on 2nd, 3rd and 4th, ratios 2.98:1, 2.02:1, 1.34:1, 1:1; 1952 automatic optional; 1953 automatic standard on LHD; 1954 automatic standard on RHD, ratios 3.82:1, 2.63:1, 1.45:1, 1:1
Clutch: 11″ heavy type
Final drive: 3.72:1; 1952 3.41:1 optional; 1954 3.41:1 std.
Suspension: Front, independent coil springs, hydraulic dampers; Rear, half-elliptic springs with controllable hydraulic dampers
Steering: Cam and roller
Brakes: Front, hydraulic; Rear, mechanical. Mechanical servo assist
GENERAL
Wheelbase: .... 120″
Track: Front: .... 56½″
Rear: .... 58⅝″
Tires: .... 6.50 × 15″
Weight: .... Approx. 4250 lbs.
Number produced: 2320

R type: *Park Ward fixedhead coupe.*

R type: *Park Ward drophead coupe.*

R type: *H.J. Mulliner two-door Lightweight saloon.*

R type: *Hooper two-door saloon.*

R-Type Continental 1952-1955

16

The R-type Continental is considered by most knowledgeable collectors to be among the half dozen or so truly important automobiles to have been built since World War II. It was claimed to be the fastest four-passenger saloon of its time, and at a price approaching $18,000 in 1952, was among the most expensive.

In 1950 Chief Project Engineer H.I.F. Evernden and stylist J.P. Blatchley were given the assignment of creating a lightweight, aerodynamic Bentley saloon which would offer rapid acceleration and excellent handling qualities while carrying four people in comfort to speeds of approximately 120 MPH, no mean feat at that time, when considering that few outright sportscars offered such performance. Rolls-Royce had been carrying out experiments in aerodynamic design as early as 1933, with Evernden heading the Streamline Bentley Mark II project. He was instrumental in the creation in 1938 of the original Corniche which was the prototype for the Bentley Mark V. Lessons learned in these exercises were brought into play when designing the new Bentley Continental. It was known that to achieve approximately 20% higher speed than the standard car, the gear ratio would have to be increased. And this in turn would require a lighter body with a lower drag co-efficient while retaining traditional Bentley appearance.

H.J. Mulliner, which had produced some aerodynamic, lightweight bodies on the Mark VI chassis, was commissioned to construct the prototype. The entire body, window frames, seat frames, and bumpers were made of light alloy, resulting in a body which weighed only 750 pounds. This body mounted on the chassis gave a weight of only 3750 pounds for the complete car. The prototype was completed by August of 1951 and was to become known as Olga, because of her registration number OLG490. This car was initially fitted with a 2.79:1 rear axle ratio and a gearbox which was overdriven on top gear. While in France for speed testing it was realized that this combination did not suit the RPM range offered by the engine. The axle ratio was changed to one of 3.07:1, still higher than the standard chassis, and the overdrive gearbox was replaced by one with a direct-ratio top gear. With this combination fitted, the Automobile Club de France recorded an average speed of 118.75 MPH for five laps with the best single lap of 119.75. This prototype is now, and has been for many years, in the capable hands of Stanley Sedgwick, Patron and President Emeritus of the Bentley Drivers Club.

When the Continental went into production it was for export only, and the first 32 cars were delivered away from England. The fourth production car, BC4A, was purchased by that

Investment Rating: 9

great American sportsman Briggs Cunningham, who still owns it today. Mr. Cunningham is quoted as stating that of all the fine cars in his stable, the R-type Continental is his favorite—high praise indeed! This kind of response is not surprising to anyone who has been fortunate enough to drive one of these remarkable cars. Upon my first sampling of one I was amazed to see 90 MPH coming up on the speedometer in third gear without a sign of strain, and there was yet more on tap.

Upon introduction of the model and through the A, B, and C chassis series, a 4½ litre engine was used. In July, 1954 the engine displacement grew to 4.9 litres and propelled the D and E series cars. Handling and braking are good by today's standards and were remarkable in the early fifties.

Of the 208 R-type Continentals produced all but 15 were fitted with the H.J. Mulliner two-door saloon body. The remaining 15 were bodied as follows: Park Ward produced 4 drophead and 2 fixedhead coupes; 5 were bodied by Franay in France, 3 by Graber in Switzerland and one by Farina in Italy. The Mulliner saloons varied in detail specifications depending upon the purchaser's requirements. Detailed information on any specific car is available in Stanley Sedgwick's fine booklet, "Bentley R-type Continental."

Lefthand drive was available commencing with the eighth production car, BC8LA. BC connotes Bentley Continental and the L preceeding the series letter A, indicates lefthand drive. The R-type Continental is perhaps the only post-war Rolls-Royce automobile which is equally valuable in right or lefthand drive on the North American Continent. The lefthand drive version came with a column mounted manual shift in 11 cars, while 23 examples utilized a central mounted floor shift. Of the right drive cars, 127 of them featured the righthand floor shift as was standard practice in most Rolls-Royce and Bentleys, while only 5 RHD cars used the rather awkward center shift. Automatic transmission became an option with the D series; 33 right and 9 left drive cars were so equipped. Generally speaking, the right drive, right shift combination is the most smoothly operating, but each person has his own preference and prices are not particularly affected one way or the other. Again, condition is the factor which determines price and value.

Excluding the Phantom IV, the R-type Continental is perhaps the most collectible post-war car produced by Rolls-Royce. Prices have soared in the past ten years, from figures of around $10,000 in the early seventies to four times that amount and more today.

To drive one of these cars is an experience which no connoisseur of fine automobiles should miss.

ENGINE

Type: F-head inline six cylinder

Bore & stroke, displacement: 3⅝″×4½″, 4566cc; 1954 3¾″×4½″, 4887cc

Compression ratio: 7.27:1; 7.10:1, 7.20:1, 7.25:1

Carburetion: Twin HD8 2″ S.U.s

CHASSIS AND DRIVETRAIN

Transmission: 4-speed manual, synchro on 2nd, 3rd and 4th, ratios 2.67:1, 1.54:1, 1.21:1, 1:1; Automatic optional from BC1D, ratios 3.82:1, 2.63:1, 1.45:1, 1:1

Clutch: 11″ heavy type

Final drive: 3.07:1

Suspension: Front, independent coil springs, hydraulic dampers, anti-roll bar; Rear, half-elliptic springs with controllable hydraulic dampers

Steering: Cam and roller

Brakes: Front, hydraulic; Rear, mechanical. Mechanical servo assist

GENERAL

Wheelbase: . . . . 120″

Track: Front: . . . . 56½″

Rear: . . . . 58½″

Tires: . . . . 6.50×16″ India Speed Specials

Weight: . . . . Approx. 3800 lbs.

Number produced: 208

R type Continental: the prototype R type Continental known as Olga for her British registration number OLG490.

R type Continental: all but 15 of the 208 produced wore this H.J. Mulliner streamline saloon body.

R ***type Continental:*** *a rare variation by Franay of Paris. Chassis BC 51 LC. There are many subtle differences when compared to the H.J. Mulliner version. Franay also produced a 2-door notch-back design.*

R type Continental: *Park Ward drophead coupe. Although this handsome body appeared with some frequency on S1 Continentals only four were erected upon the R type Continental chassis.*

R type Continental: *Pinin Farina's sole effort in creating coachwork for the R type Continental. Chassis BC49C.*

SI CONTINENTAL

1955-1959

17

The introduction of the new S series put an end to the R-type and with it of course, the well-received R Continental. Thus it was that in October 1955 an S series of Continentals appeared. Mechanically it offered an engine compression ratio of 7.25:1 compared with 6.6:1 for the standard model, a higher rear axle ratio of 2.92:1, smaller diameter high-performance tires, and the option of a four-speed synchromesh transmission. Few customers ordered the manual gearbox and by 1957 it was no longer offered. Consequently, a manual shift SI Continental is today a rare and desirable variation. In 1956 the carburetors were enlarged from 1¾ ″ to 2 ″ and compression raised to 8:1. These changes worked so well that in 1957, U.S. delivery cars, both standard and Continental, were similarly upgraded and in 1958 all models were produced to these specifications.

The bodies fitted to the Continental chassis were lightweight to achieve the desired performance and of sporting appearance. H.J. Mulliner continued to offer the streamline two-door "fastback" saloon, albeit in an updated form for the new chassis. The front-wing line no longer dipped below the door-handle as it swept back to meet the rear wing. A scallop was incorporated into the side of the rear wing and the spats, which were no longer in vogue, were deleted. The tail lights that Mulliner fitted at this time are particularly handsome and their design is among the cleanest seen on any post-war cars.

Park Ward offered the fixedhead and drophead coupe bodies which they had fitted to a very few R-type Continentals. Minor changes included raising the position of the door-handles and the fuel filler door, eliminating the chrome trim which extended back from the tops of the headlights, and the use of different tail lights. Park Ward later modified the "greenhouse" portion of the fixedhead coupe, a change that can readily be seen in the accompanying photos. In mid-1957 H.J. Mulliner introduced a body style which is considered to be among the finest post-war work produced by that firm, the Flying Spur sports saloon. It offered beautifully balanced lines and a very handsome appearance, while adding the convenience of four doors, yet the weight is comparable to their two-door saloon. This body proved so popular that it was continued through the series 2 and 3 Continentals with a few being fitted to the CSC series of Silver Cloud IIIs as well. Other coachbuilders, including James Young, Hooper, Graber and Franay, made a few bodies for the SI Continental, but of the 430 chassis produced, Park Ward and J.H. Mulliner bodied the vast majority, with the total for the two firms approximating 400.

Investment Rating: 8

S1 **Continental:** *H.J. Mulliner streamline sports saloon.*

ENGINE

Type: F-head inline six cylinder

Bore & stroke, displacement: 3¾″ × 4½″, 4887 cc

Compression ratio: 7.25:1; 1956 8:1

Carburetion: Twin HD6 S.U.s; 1956 twin HD8 S.U.s

CHASSIS AND DRIVETRAIN

Transmission: 4-speed automatic, ratios 3.82:1, 2.63:1, 1.45:1, 1:1; 4-speed manual available, but few built

Final drive: 2.92:1 or 3.07:1

Suspension: Front, independent coil springs, unequal length wishbones, hydraulic dampers and anti-roll bar; Rear, semi-elliptic springs, controllable hydraulic dampers, Z type anti-roll bar

Steering: Cam and roller, 1956 power assist optional

Brakes: Front, self-adjusting hydraulic; Rear, combined hydraulic and mechanical, mechanical servo assist

GENERAL

Wheelbase:	123″
Track: Front:	58″
Rear:	60″
Tires:	7.60 × 15″ or 8.00 × 15″
Weight:	Approx. 4000 lbs.
Number produced:	430

__S1 Continental:__ Park Ward fixedhead coupe.

__S1 Continental:__ H.J. Mulliner Flying Spur sports saloon.

S1 Continental: *Park Ward fixed-head coupe. Note quarter-lights and rear window have become larger on late versions for improved visability.*

S1 Continental: *Park Ward drophead coupe.*

S1 Continental: *Hooper exhibited this model at the 1958 London Show. Fortunately few were ordered.*

S2 Continental

1959-1962

18

The V8 engine was a natural for the Continental series. As had been standard Rolls-Royce practice, horsepower figures were not released. The Company simply stated that the horsepower was "adequate." But to anyone having the opportunity to drive one of the new cars it was clear that the power was more than adequate. The 6¼ litre V8 appeared on the Continental chassis in the same state of tune as that fitted to the standard car; the chassis specifications differed only in the Continental's slightly higher rear axle ratio and the use of special high-speed tires. It was felt that these changes along with the lightweight bodies that would be mounted on this chassis would provide performance which would satisfy the customers' needs, and such was the case.

The late fifties and early sixties were not the happiest of times for automobile body styling, both in the U.S. and abroad. Even H.J. Mulliner succumb to what it assumed must be the fashion of the day with a two-door saloon which sported fins on the rear wings and recessed "eyebrows" housing the parking lights in the front wings. Fortunately only about six of these were produced before the design was revised and became what is considered by some to be the most handsome body fitted to the S2 Continental.

H.J. Mulliner continued to offer the popular Flying Spur four-door saloon. The bonnet was lengthened and the rear deck was made somewhat longer and flatter in profile. The boot lid opening now extended down nearer the rear bumper to facilitate easier loading. Park Ward, undaunted by their unsuccessful efforts at a rather slabsided design on the Mark VI, once again produced a slabsided body, this time in drophead coupe form. James Young created a four-door six-light saloon which is sometimes mistakenly referred to as a Flying Spur, Mulliner's term exclusively. This car is a very satisfactory alternative to the Spur if one desires a four-door Continental.

The S2 Continental was prone to the same mechanical teething problems as occured in the early Silver Cloud IIs and the S2 Bentleys. Please refer to that chapter for details. The four-speed automatic transmission was used exclusively; the manual gearbox had not been an option since 1957. The brakes were standard Rolls-Royce, hydraulic front with hydraulic and mechanical operation at the rear. The transmission-driven servo-assisted brakes were retained on the V8 cars and continued in use until the introduction of the three-speed automatic gearbox in the Silver Shadow/T-type series.

The S2 Continental, with its higher performance and coachbuilt luxury, provides an interesting alternative for those perhaps willing to spend a bit extra for a more exclusive and sporting statement than that which is made by the standard steel models.

Investment Rating: 7-8

*S**2 Continental:** H.J. Mulliner two-door saloon.*

ENGINE
Type: Overhead valve V8
Bore & stroke, displacement: 4.1″ × 3.6″, 6230cc
Compression ratio: 8:1
Carburetion: Twin HD6 S.U.s

CHASSIS AND DRIVETRAIN
Transmission: 4-speed automatic, ratios 3.82:1, 2.63:1, 1.45:1, 1:1
Final drive: 2.92:1
Suspension: Front, independent coil springs, unequal length wishbones, hydraulic dampers and anti-roll bar; Rear, semi-elliptic springs, controllable hydraulic dampers, single radius rod
Steering: Power assisted cam and roller
Brakes: Front, self-adjusting hydraulic; Rear, combined hydraulic and mechanical, mechanical servo assist, finned drums

GENERAL
Wheelbase: .... 123″
Track: Front: .... 58½″
Rear: .... 60″
Tires: .... 8.00×15″
Weight: .... Approx. 4250 lbs.
Number produced: 388

S2 Continental: H.J. Mulliner two-door saloon. An unfortunate variation on a handsome design.

S2 Continental: Park Ward drophead coupe.

H.J. Mulliner factory: *Bentley S2 Continentals in the process of completion.*

H.J. Mulliner factory *circa 1960. S2 Continental fitted with trade plates awaits roadtest. Note on left the only Hooper bodied Phantom V being prepared for delivery.*

S3 CONTINENTAL

1962-1966

19

As the years passed, the memory of Bentley's great pre-war racing exploits faded. The name no longer carried a strong performance image as it had in the past. Bentley was now thought of in much the same way as was Rolls-Royce; a smooth, silent, luxury automobile. The S3 Continental reflected this notion, for the car no longer had a higher rear axle ratio than the standard model and virtually all other specifications were now the same. What it offered was a somewhat smaller frontal area with lighter, more aerodynamic coachwork to give it added performance. And make no mistake, the Continental provides genuine performance and will still shame many fine cars encountered today. The market for a high performance Bentley had simply become so small that it was not in the best corporate interest to produce a specially tuned chassis for so few cars. Also, the Company had the introduction of the long awaited Silver Shadow/T-type in sight and all efforts were being channeled in that direction.

Mulliner-Park Ward, by this time merged into one company under the parent Rolls-Royce Limited, offered coachbuilt elegance with the Flying Spur and also a revised edition of the slabsided Park Ward design from the S2 Continental. This model was now available as either a fixedhead or a drophead coupe and featured four headlights, as had become the norm for most cars by that time. At $26,357 for the Flying Spur, and $26,141 and $26,070 respectively for the fixedhead and drophead coupes, these cars were nearly $10,000 more than the standard S3 which listed for $16,721. The exclusivity of the Continental however was a thing of the past, as these bodies could now be ordered on the standard Rolls-Royce Silver Cloud III chassis.

Perhaps the rarest body to be found on the S3 Continental is the Mulliner two-door saloon, originally designed for the S2 series. A very limited number of these were made utilizing four headlights in place of the two as had been used previously. Fewer than a dozen are thought to have been produced.

While the S3 Continental was not of course a true sportscar, it was the last of the sporting Bentleys until the Mulsanne Turbo was announced and it still offers a wonderful combination of performance and elan.

Investment Rating: 7-8

S3 **Continental:** *H.J. Mulliner two-door saloon.*

ENGINE
Type: Overhead valve V8
Bore & stroke, displacement: 4.1″×3.6″, 6230cc
Compression ratio: 9:1 or 8:1 available
Carburetion: Twin HD8 S.U.s
CHASSIS AND DRIVETRAIN
Transmission: 4-speed automatic, ratios 3.82:1, 2.63:1, 1.45:1, 1:1
Final drive: 3.08:1
Suspension: Front, independent coil springs, unequal length wishbones, hydraulic dampers and anti-roll bar; Rear, semi-elliptic springs, controllable hydraulic dampers, single radius rod
Steering: Power assisted cam and roller
Brakes: Front, self-adjusting hydraulic; Rear, combined hydraulic and mechanical, mechanical servo assist, finned drums, two separate hydraulic systems and master cylinders
GENERAL
Wheelbase: . . . . 123″
Track: Front: . . . . 58½″
Rear: . . . . 60″
Tires: . . . . 8.20×15″
Weight: . . . . Approx. 4250 lbs.
Number produced: 296

S3 Continental: *H.J. Mulliner Flying Spur sports saloon with smaller than normal rear quarter lights.*

S3 Continental: *Park Ward fixedhead coupe.*

S3 **Continental:** *Park Ward drop-head coupe.*

MULSANNE TURBO

1982-PRESENT

20

While this Bentley is not called a "Continental," it is the first Bentley in nearly twenty years in the tradition of that great series, and surely belongs in this section of the book. It is a model unique unto itself and not merely a product of "badge engineering."

The Mulsanne Turbo conjures up visions of Sir Henry Birkin driving his supercharged 4½ Litre Bentley against the Mercedes challenge at Le Mans in 1930, but perhaps can be more readily likened to the 6½ and 8 Litre Bentleys of that time; smooth, silent and fast as opposed to thundering and raucous. It must surely be among the most desirable and exciting new cars offered in a decade, and while as of this writing it is not available in Japan, Australia or on the North American Continent, the rest of the world has the opportunity, albeit an expensive one, to sample high performance luxury motoring of another era.

The Mulsanne Turbo is based on the Bentley Mulsanne four-door saloon and is distinguished by a radiator shell painted body color and not chromium plated, a leather rimmed steering wheel, dual exhaust tips exiting at the right rear, and discreet Turbo badges. The real excitement lurks under the bonnet, for there lives the Garrett AiResearch turbocharger, fed from both exhaust banks and controlled by a wastegate regulating the amount of exhaust gasses fed into the unit.

Special pistons utilizing cast-in steel webs are fitted to accommodate the compression, which varies from the basic 8:1 to 11:1 at full boost, as well as the resulting higher temperature created. Spent exhaust gasses exit via nickel-iron manifolds and an exhaust system with 50% greater output capacity than that of the standard model. The transmission torque converter and some of the suspension components are also of increased specification to handle the added power put through them. All of this adds up to a luxuriously comfortable and quiet four-door saloon weighing nearly 5000 pounds yet capable of accelerating from 0 to 60 MPH in a mere 7.4 seconds, with a top speed, as reported by MOTOR SPORT in the June 1982 issue, in excess of 140 MPH.

One can only speculate about the investment potential of new models. But taking into consideration the performance offered by the Mulsanne Turbo, especially in this era of lack-lustre, economy oriented automobiles, and the exclusivity of a car available only in very limited numbers, I feel secure stating that this car is destined to become a modern classic.

Investment Rating: 8-9

Mulsanne Turbo: *easily identifiable by body color, painted radiator shell.*

ENGINE
Type: Overhead valve V8
Bore & stroke, displacement: 4.1″ × 3.9″, 6750cc
Compression ratio: 8:1; 11:1 with full turbo boost
Carburetion: 4A1 Solex four choke

CHASSIS AND DRIVETRAIN
Transmission: 3-speed automatic with uprated torque converter, ratios 2.48:1, 1.48:1, 1:1
Final drive: 2.70:1
Suspension: Front, independent by lower wishbone, compliant controlled upper levers, coil springs, telescopic dampers; Rear, independent by semi-trailing arms, suspension struts, gas springs; Front and rear anti-roll bars, automatic ride height control, uprated half shafts
Steering: Power assisted rack and pinion
Brakes: Four wheel power assisted 11″ discs, front discs ventilated

GENERAL
Wheelbase: . . . . 120.5″
Track: Front: . . . . 60.5″
Rear: . . . . 60.5″
Tires: . . . . Avon 235/70 VR 15″
Weight: . . . . Approx. 4950 lbs.
Number produced: . . . . N/A

Mulsanne Turbo: *engine compartment.*

Special Interest

21

In this "catch-all" chapter are shown a wide assortment of interesting bodies, ranging from one-off designs by well-known coachbuilding firms to cars which have had existing coachwork modified to suit an owner's particular requirements, or simply to satisfy a desire for something different. Also shown are cars which have been prepared for special utility assignments or for competition.

While some may not condone the use of these cars for other than "conventional purposes," it must be remembered that these sturdy automobiles have been used over the years for everything from armored cars during World War I to tow trucks. Some even have been outfitted to run on tracks as rail cars.

Regardless of one's views on modified coachwork, I am confident that the following photos will be of interest.

***S**ilver Shadow:* *Coachwork has been transformed into a 4-door cabriolet. Note rear doors are hinged at the back.*

Corniche: A shortened 2-seater convertible with S3 type headlights.

Silver Shadow: *An individually styled example featuring a side reveal with canework, spats and an S1, S2 style front-end treatment.*

Phantom V: *What started life as a Park Ward 7 Passenger Limousine was decapitated to become this immense convertible.*

Silver Cloud I: *Hooper modified a standard steel saloon into this unusual two-seater fixedhead coupe.*

Silver Wraith: *Charles K. Bowers archives indicate that Hooper was responsible for this estate wagon remodel of a Park Ward limousine.*

Silver Wraith: *An "Estate Lorry" conversion by Classic Coachworks in California to what was once a hearse. This should strike a familiar note to readers of John D. MacDonald.*

Silver Shadow: *A similar conversion on an early Shadow.*

Silver Shadow: *Classic Coachworks is also responsible for this handsome Estate wagon on the long wheelbase chassis.*

Mk. VI: *Hooper-built utility body.*

Mk. VI: *A shooting brake by an unknown coachbuilder on what appears to be an early chassis.*

Mk. VI: *Some of the first Harold Radford efforts resulted in fully coachbuilt bodies. This early example is a two-door estate wagon.*

Mk VI: *The fully-coachbuilt 4-door saloon by Radford on the big-bore Mk. VI chassis featured unusual treatment to the spats and numerous surprises including seats which reclined into a usable bed as shown below and a versatile hatch-back as pictured on the Silver Dawn. Virtually any amenity could be fitted such as cooking implements, picnic table with stools and even a water closet!*

Mk. VI: *Interior shot of the Radford estate wagon shows the rear seat folded, note also a luggage restrictor which in its standing position prevents luggage from striking the seat backs. An umbrella holder can be seen behind the seats.*

Silver Wraith: *WZB36 Inskip drophead coupe. Only two examples of this flamboyant design were produced by this New York based firm.*

Silver Dawn: *Harold Radford did many conversions to standard steel coachwork, among them this hatchback with provisions for picnicking.*

Silver Wraith: *An elegant 4-door cabriolet by Hooper & Co. for the fabled Turkish industrialist Nubar Gulbenkian. It was by his commission that Hooper built some of the most outlandishly styled bodies seen on Rolls-Royce chassis. This example features Perspex-covered headlights and a fully-disappearing power-operated top.*

Silver Cloud I: *Chassis SED179, Freestone & Webb erected this unusual and controversial two-seater drophead coupe on a Bentley S1 chassis as well as the SCI illustrated in these two photos.*

***Above is the Silver Wraith** in which Mike Couper competed in the 1950 Monte Carlo Rally. Below is his 1951, Mk. VI Bentley entry with pivoting cornering lamp and headlight wipers.*

***Mk. VI:** Freestone and Webb special saloon with very unusual fender treatment.*

Mk. VI: *A less than handsome design by Windovers on an early chassis, B95AJ, with what appears to be a tool locker in the front wing.*

Mk. VI: *Another early chassis with a 4-seater sunroof coupe by an unknown coachbuilder.*

Silver Wraith: *In 1949 Hooper & Co. created this "New Look" saloon with rather bulbous tail section.*

RESALE PRICES

1972-1982

22

The following figures are average ASKING prices, compiled from cars offered in The Rolls-Royce Owners' Club publication *The Flying Lady* and *Hemmings Motor News* during the years listed. The cars used in attaining these figures appeared to be solid, usable examples of the marque, fitted with saloon or limousine coachwork in the case of the Bentley Continentals, Silver Wraith and Phantom Vs. All other models represent asking prices when fitted with standard steel coachwork. Convertibles and one-off body designs have been excluded from this survey and can command much higher prices in most cases. Cars which were obviously overpriced and those appearing to be in poor condition were not used.

It must be remembered that these are ASKING prices, and often the sums realized are lower, but it is felt that this listing will be useful in acquiring a feel for the cars and the market trends.

ROLLS-ROYCE PRICES 1972–1982

	S WRAITH	S DAWN	S CLOUD I	S CLOUD II	S CLOUD III	P V
1972	$ 9,450	$ 5,700	$ 8,000	$10,600	$13,166	$ *
1973	11,730	9,350	10,150	9,812	16,500	35,000*
1974	14,244	15,833	10,950	13,922	15,750	40,750
1975	16,218	14,250	12,604	15,980	19,722	44,375
1976	20,321	18,250	14,700	14,737	19,562	63,333
1977	22,785	21,375	14,833	18,666	23,212	66,666
1978	20,156	20,583	18,243	18,409	21,766	38,547
1979	20,932	19,866	17,619	21,209	28,434	57,523
1980	25,856	28,469	22,578	23,404	27,125	70,000
1981	29,260	26,535	25,284	23,780	30,265	76,083
1982	23,705	28,625	24,961	31,065	32,949	85,725

BENTLEY PRICES 1972–1982

	MK. VI-R	S1	S2	S3	R-CONTI	S-CONTI
1972	$ 4,118	$ 6,016	$ 5,666	$ *	$ 7,500*	$13,500
1973	4,883	4,950*	7,400	10,450*	*	19,800*
1974	6,455	5,842	8,250*	*	*	11,400*
1975	6,890	8,157	12,375	7,750*	*	17,333
1976	7,287	9,514	13,000	15,666	*	22,250
1977	10,090	11,700	12,500	18,500*	17,000*	17,450
1978	9,881	10,395	11,918	14,764	25,500*	25,015
1979	10,760	12,391	19,470	16,728	24,500*	26,645
1980	13,804	15,193	18,792	20,166	45,750	31,914
1981	14,464	16,705	19,114	15,650	48,000*	33,247
1982	13,723	18,142	18,244	23,381	39,500	31,938

*Indicates zero to three examples were offered for sale during that year and therefore the price shown, if any, may not be truly representative.

NORTH AMERICAN ROLLS-ROYCE DEALERS

23

ARIZONA

MAX OF SWITZERLAND
6913 East McDowell Road
Scottsdale (85257)
Phone: (602) 945-4545

MATTHEWS
MOTOR COMPANY
4901 North Oracle Road
P.O. Box 27878
Tucson (85726-7878)
Phone: (602) 888-7900

CALIFORNIA

ROLLS-ROYCE OF BEVERLY
HILLS, LTD.
9018 Wilshire Boulevard
Beverly Hills (90211)
Phone: (213) 659-4050

TERRY YORK MOTOR
CARS, LTD.
15800 Ventura Boulevard
Encino (91436)
Phone: (213) 990-9870

FRESNO DODGE/
ROLLS-ROYCE
6162 North Blackstone Avenue
Fresno (93710)
Phone: (209) 431-4000

BRITISH MOTORS OF
MONTEREY, INC.
777 Del Monte Avenue
Monterey (93940)
Phone: (408) 373-3041

ROY CARVER, INC.
1540 Jamboree Road
P.O. Box 7180
Newport Beach (92660-0180)
Phone: (714) 640-6444

PETER EPSTEEN, LTD.
68-131 Highway 111
Palm Springs (92262)
Phone: (714) 328-8981

PETER SATORI CO., LTD.
285-325 West Colorado Blvd.
Pasadena (91105)
Phone: (213) 681-8123

SWIFT DODGE
6250 Florin Road
P.O. Box 9927
Sacramento (95823)
Phone: (916) 422-4300

ROY CARVER, INC., OF
SAN DIEGO
D.B.A. SAN DIEGO, LTD.
9010 Miramar Road
P.O. Box 26266
San Diego (92126)
Phone: (714) 578-8600

BRITISH MOTOR CAR
DISTRIBUTORS, LTD.
901 Van Ness Avenue
San Francisco (94109)
Phone: (415) 776-7700

SMYTHE BUICK, INC.
D.B.A. SMYTHE EUROPEAN
4500 Stevens Creek Boulevard
San Jose (95129)
Phone: (408) 985-8600

COLORADO

ROYAL CARRIAGE WORKS
AT D.T.C. INC.
D.B.A. ROYAL CARRIAGE
WORKS AT MY GARAGE, INC.
455 Broadway
Denver (80203)
Phone: (303) 778-1766

CONNECTICUT

HOFFMAN OLDSMOBILE, INC.
700 Connecticut Boulevard
East Hartford (06108)
Phone: (203) 528-6555

IMPORTED CARS OF
GREENWICH, INC.
217 West Putnam Avenue
Greenwich (06830)
Phone: (203) 869-2850

SCOTT OLDSMOBILE, INC.
Route No. 44 Albany Turnpike
West Simsbury (06092)
Phone: (203) 651-3371

FLORIDA

LAUDERDALE MOTOR CAR
CORPORATION
407 North Federal Highway
Fort Lauderdale (33301)
Phone: (305) 764-5881

VAL WARD IMPORTS, INC.
8700 S. Tamiami Trail
Fort Myers (33907)
Phone: (813) 939-4616

GREGG MOTOR CARS, INC.
10231 Atlantic Blvd.
Jacksonville (32211)
Phone: (904) 724-1080

BRAMAN MOTORS, INC.
2020 Biscayne Boulevard
P.O. Box 967
Miami (33137)
Phone: (305) 576-6900

LOUIS VOLKSWAGEN, INC.
6363 East Colonial Drive
Orlando (32807)
Phone: (305) 277-7220

SCARRITT MOTORS, INC.
555 34th Street, South
St. Petersburg (33711)
Phone: (813) 327-3700

ROYAL MOTORCAR
CORPORATION
1314 South Dixie Highway
West Palm Beach (33401)
Phone: (305) 659-1314

GEORGIA

MITCHELL MOTORS, INC.
5675 Peachtree Industrial
Boulevard
Chamblee (30341)
Phone: (404) 458-5111

HAWAII

CONTINENTAL CARS, LTD.
1072 Young Street
Honolulu (96814)
Phone: (808) 526-3258

ILLINOIS

WORDEN-MARTIN, INC.
100 Carriage Center
2003 S. Neil Street
Champaign (61820)
Phone: (217) 352-7901

LOEBER IMPORTERS, LTD.
5625 North Broadway
Chicago (60660)
Phone: (312) 728-5000

LOEBER IMPORTERS, LTD.
1111 North Clark Street
Chicago (60610)
Phone: (312) 944-0500

CONTINENTAL MOTORS, INC.
420 E. Ogden Avenue
Hinsdale (60521)
Phone: (312) 655-3535

INDIANA

ALBERS ROLLS-ROYCE
360 South First Street
Zionsville (46077)
Phone: Sales (317) 873-2360
Service (317) 873-2460

KENTUCKY

TOM PAYETTE BUICK, INC.
3700 Frankfort Avenue
Louisville (40207)
Phone: (502) 895-2451

LOUISIANA

ESTES CADILLAC, INC.
727 Baronne Street
New Orleans (70113)
Phone: (504) 581-7585

MARYLAND

EURO MOTORCARS
BETHESDA, INC.
4800 Elm Street
Bethesda (20814)
Phone: (301) 986-8800

LEE OLDSMOBILE, INC.
D.B.A. GLADDING
ROLLS-ROYCE
7370 Crain Highway
Glen Burnie (21061)
Phone: (301) 761-9393

MASSACHUSETTS

FOREIGN MOTORS WEST, INC.
253 North Main Street
(Route No 27)
Natick (01760)
Phone: (617) 235-9096

MICHIGAN

TAMAROFF BUICK OPEL INC
D.B.A. TAMAROFF
BUICK-DMC-HONDA
28585 Telegraph Road
Southfield (48034)
Phone: (313) 353-1300

MINNESOTA

SEARS IMPORTED
AUTOS, INC.
13500 Wayzata Boulevard
Minnetonka (55343)
Phone: (612) 546-5301

MISSOURI

CHARLES SCHMITT AND
COMPANY
3500 South Kingshighway
Boulevard
St. Louis (63139)
Phone: (314) 352-9100

MAJOR CADILLAC CO., INC.
3200 Main
Kansas City (64111)
Phone: (816) 756-3300

NEVADA

CUTTER MOTOR CARS
2333 South Decatur Boulevard
Las Vegas (89102)
Phone: (702) 871-1010

MODERN CLASSIC MOTORS
3225 Mill Street
Reno (89501)
Phone: (702) 323-4169

NEW JERSEY

IMPORTED MOTOR CAR
COMPANY
34 Valley Road
Montclair (07042)
Phone: (201) 746-4500

NEW MEXICO

PERFECTION MOTOR
CAR, LTD.
6012 Academy Road N.E.
Albuquerque (87109)
Phone: (505) 822-8500

NEW YORK

RALLYE MOTORS, INC.
20 Cedar Swamp Road
Glen Cove (11542)
Phone: (516) 671-4622

MARTY CADILLAC
OLDSMOBILE
271 North Bedford Road
Mount Kisco (10549)
Phone: (914) 241-3800

GEORGE HAUG
COMPANY, INC.
(Service Only)
517 East 73rd Street
New York (10021)
Phone: (212) 288-0173

PARK WARD
MOTORS, INC.
301 East 57th Street
New York (10022)
Phone: (212) 688-7112

PIEHLER PONTIAC CORP.
1560 Lake Avenue
Rochester (14615)
Phone: (716) 458-4540

NORTH CAROLINA

TRANSCO, INC.
1800 N. Main Street
High Point (27262)
Phone: (919) 885-5171

OHIO

WILLIAMS FORD SALES, INC.
9260 Montgomery Road
Cincinnati (45242)
Phone: (513) 891-0500

QUA BUICK & LEASING
28000 Chagrin Boulevard
Woodmere Village (44122)
Phone: (216) 831-7177

LEN IMMKE BUICK, INC.
31 South Fifth Street
Columbus (43215)
Phone: (614) 228-1701

OKLAHOMA

JACKIE COOPER
IMPORTS, INC.
9505 North May Avenue
Oklahoma (73120)
Phone: (405) 755-3600

SIGGI GRIMM MOTORS, INC.
2007 East 11th Street
Tulsa (74104)
Phone: (918) 582-1151

OREGON

MONTE'S MOTORS COMPANY
D.B.A. MONTE SHELTON
MOTOR COMPANY
1638 West Burnside Street
P.O. Box 5545
Portland (97228)
Phone: (503) 224-3232

PENNSYLVANIA

KEENAN MOTORS, INC.
3900 North Broad Street
Philadelphia (19140)
Phone: (215) 223-4600

ASCOT IMPORTED CARS, INC.
418 Walnut Street
Sewickly (15143)
Phone: (412) 761-9310

HENRY PAUL CADILLAC, INC.
325 East Lancaster Avenue
Wayne (19087)
Phone: (215) 687-0800

RHODE ISLAND

STEINGOLD PONTIAC
CORPORATION, INC.
766 Broadway
Pawtucket (02862)
Phone: (401) 723-4700

SOUTH CAROLINA

DICK DYER &
ASSOCIATES, INC.
5717 Two Notch Road
Columbia (29204)
Phone: (803) 786-2010

TENNESSEE

AUTORAMA, INC.
2950 Airways Boulevard
Memphis (38130)
Phone: (901) 345-6211

SUPERIOR MOTORS, INC.
630 Murfreesboro Road
Nashville (37210)
Phone: (615) 254-5641

TEXAS

OVERSEAS MOTORS OF
DALLAS
7018 Lemmon Avenue
Dallas (75209)
Phone: Sales (214) 358-1446

SUN DATSUN, INC.
5855 Montana Avenue
El Paso (79925)
Phone: (915) 772-1488

OVERSEAS MOTORS CORP.
OF FORT WORTH
2824 White Settlement Road
Fort Worth (76107)
Phone: (817) 332-4181

McGINNIS CADILLAC, INC.
12221 Katy Freeway
Houston (77079)
Phone: (713) 496-8700

KENT BIEL BUICK, GMC, INC.
500 East Miracle Mile
McAllen (78501)
Phone: (512) 687-5286

THE JOHN J. SCHALER III
COLLECTION, INC.
D.B.A. THE SCHALER
COLLECTION
8383 West Highway No. 80
Midland (79701)
Phone: (915) 563-0594

UTAH

KEN GARFF FOREIGN
CARS, INC.
D.B.A. KEN GARFF IMPORTS
525 South State Street
Salt Lake City (84111)
Phone: (801) 521-6604

VIRGINIA

DOMINION
ROLLS-ROYCE, LTD.
6517 West Broad Street
Richmond (23230)
Phone: (804) 288-3171

BROWN'S TYSON'S CORNER
DODGE, INC.
8606 Leesburg Pike
Vienna (22180)
Phone: (703) 893-2670

WISCONSIN

UPTOWN MOTORS, INC.
2111 North Mayfair Road
Milwaukee (53226)
Phone: (414) 771-9000

SUPPLIERS OF PARTS AND SERVICES

24

Below is a list naming some suppliers of parts and services for Rolls-Royce and Bentley automobiles. This in no way constitutes an endorsement, it is merely provided for your convenience.

ALBERS ROLLS-ROYCE
360 S. First St.
Zionsville, IN 46077
(317) 873-2360
Parts.

BILL HIRSCH
396 Littleton Ave.
Newark, NJ 07103
(201) 642-2404
Carpet, leather, paint.

BOB'S AUTO PARTS
Rt. 9W
Kingston, NY 12401
(914) 336-6330
Used parts.

BORLA AUTOMOTIVE INDUSTRIES, INC.
61 Java St.
Brooklyn, NY 11222
(212) 389-8700
Exhaust systems.

CLASSIC AUTO RESTORATIONS
22456 Orchard Lake Rd.
Farmington, MI 48024
(313) 477-4767
Parts.

DALE POWERS AUTOMOTIVE INC.
1811 11th Ave. N.
St. Petersburg, FL 33713
(813) 821-8883
Parts.

DONALD M. STEINERT
800 Messinger Rd.
Grants Pass, OR 97526
(503) 846-6835
Interior woodwork.

DUNNING COACHWOOD LTD.
180 Serenity Lane
Charlotte Hall, MD 20622
(301) 884-3000
Interior woodwork.

E.J. REYNOLDS
2632 E. 13th Pl.
Tulsa, OK 74104
(918) 744-0417
Head and block repair.

FOREIGN MOTORS WEST
253 N. Main St.
Natick, MA 01760
(617) 653-4323
Parts.

FOREIGN PARTS CONNECTION, INC.
2028 Coter Ave.
Westwood, CA 90025
(213) 473-7773
Used parts.

HIBERNIA AUTO RESTORATIONS INC.
Maple Terrace
Hibernia, NJ 07960
(201) 627-1882
Nitrocellulose lacquer

HILBORN MOTOR CAR INTERIORS
7025 Reseda Blvd.
Reseda, CA 91335
(213) 345-2113
Lambs wool overcarpets.

JOHN McCOMBE INC.
572 S. Nelson Rd.
Columbus, Ohio 43205
(614) 221-2563
Parts.

KNIGHT-CLARKE SERVICES
8 Bodine Ave.
Gladstone, NJ 07934
(201) 234-2930
Parts.

MARK WALLACH, LTD.
27 New St.
Nyack, NY 10960
(914) 358-8179
Interior woodwork.

R & B PARTS
4546 Palm Beach Canal Rd.
West Palm Beach, FL 33406
(305) 689-7888
Parts.

REPLACEMENT PARTS CO.
4244 Double Gate Dr.
Douglasville, GA 30135
(404) 942-8779
Rubber trim.

R R PARTS RECYCLERS, INC.
P.O. Box 4462
Glendale, CA 91202
(213) 500-7600
Parts.

SUNSHINE ENTERPRISES, INC
306 N. Missouri
Potosi, MO 63664
(314) 438-3230
Interior woodwork.

TURNER SPARES, LTD.
Box 396
Edison, NJ 08818
(201) 225-5800
Postwar parts.

THE VINTAGE GARAGE
North Brookfield, MA 01535
(617) 867-2892
Parts.

SUPPLIERS IN ENGLAND

ADAMS & OLIVER, LTD.
Ramsey Road
Warboys, Huntingdon
Cambs. PE17 2RP England
PH. 487-822488
Pre-1966 parts.

APPLEYARD OF LEEDS
Roseville Rd., Leeds 8
West Yorkshire, England
PH. 532-432731
Pre-1955 parts.

LEX MEAD
128 Bridge Road
Maidenhead, Berkshire
England
PH. 628-33188
Post-1955 parts.

WADHAM STRINGER
Woodbridge Road
Guildford, Surrey
GU1 1DX England
PH. 483-69231
Post-1955 parts.

Rolls-Royce and Bentley Clubs

25

For membership information contact the club secretary at the addresses shown below.

THE ROLLS-ROYCE OWNERS' CLUB, INC.
P.O. Box 2001
Mechanicsburg, PA 17055 USA
Telephone (717) 697-4671

THE BENTLEY DRIVERS CLUB
W.O. Bentley Memorial Building
16 Chearsley Road
Long Crendon
Aylesbury, Bucks., HP18 9AW
England
Telephone 0844 208233

THE ROLLS-ROYCE ENTHUSIASTS' CLUB
The Hunt House
High Street
Paulersbury
Northamptonshire
England

Bibliography

26

While many fine books have been written about these two marques, the books listed below will be of particular interest to those wishing to learn more about the post-war cars.

Bentley: Fifty Years of the Marque
Johnnie Green
Dalton Watson Ltd. 1969

The Rolls-Royce Motor Car
Anthony Bird and Ian Hallows
Crown Publishers, Inc. 1964

Cricklewood to Crewe
Michael Frostick
Osprey Publishing, Inc. 1980

Rolls-Royce: The Elegance Continues
Lawrence Dalton
Dalton Watson Ltd. 1971

Bentley R-Type Continental
Stanley Sedgwick
The Bentley Drivers Club 1978

The Rolls-Royce Companion
Kenneth Ullyett
Craft Publications Trust Ltd. 1969

Rolls-Royce: 75 Years of Motoring Excellence
Edward Eves
Crescent Books 1979

The Complete Book of Rolls-Royce
Michael Frostick
Libreria dell'Automobile 1980

Rolls-Royce Silver Shadow
John Bolster
Osprey Publishing, Inc. 1979

Rolls-Royce Silver Cloud
Graham Robson
Osprey Publishing, Inc. 1980

Twenty Years of Crewe Bentleys
Stanley Sedgwick
The Bentley Drivers Club

Rolls-Royce: Seven Decades of Descriptions, Reports and Road Tests in Facsimile
Chartwell Books, Inc. 1977

TAIL PIECE

ROLLS
RR
ROYCE